A Frontier Army Christmas

Compiled and Annotated by
Lori A. Cox-Paul and Dr. James W. Wengert

Nebraska State Historical Society
1996

**Sergeant Streaman and children at Fort Sill, Oklahoma
Territory.** Courtesy U.S. Army Field Artillery and Fort Sill
Museum.

Publication of this book was made possible by
The Robert F. Lute II Memorial Fund
established at the Nebraska State Historical Society Foundation.

Library of Congress Catalog Card Number: 96-070900
ISBN 0-933307-02-0

CONTENTS

San Juan Islands

Ft. Stevens

Ft. Coeur
d'Alene

Ft. Shaw

Cp. Cooke

Ft. Buford

Ft. Stevenson

Ft. Keogh

Ft. Abraham
Lincoln
Ft. Rice

Ft. Custer

Ft. Yates

Ft. C.F. Smith

Cp. Warner

Ft. Boise

Ft. Phil Kearny

Ft. McKinney

Ft. Washakie

Pine Ridge
Agency

Ft. McDermit

Ft. Fetterman

Ft. Halleck

Ft. Bridger

Ft. Laramie

Ft. Niobrara

Cp. Sheridan

Ft. Fred Steele

Ft. Robinson

Ft. Douglas

Ft. D.A. Russell

Ft. Sidney

Ft. McPherson

Ft. Crawford

Ft. Wallace

Ft. Lyon

Ft. Dodge

Ft. Union

Ft. Wingate

Ft. Whipple

Cp. Verde

Ft. McDowell

Ft. Bayard

Ft. Huachuca

Ft. Bliss

Ft. Concho

Ft. Davis

Ft. Clark

Map by Dell Darling

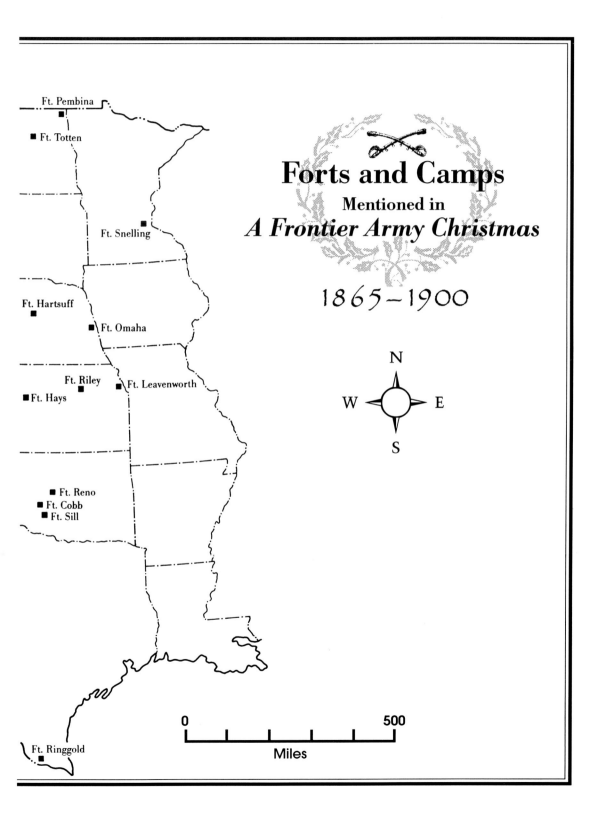

Ft. Pembina

■ Ft. Totten

Ft. Snelling

Forts and Camps
Mentioned in
A Frontier Army Christmas

1865–1900

Ft. Hartsuff
■

■ Ft. Omaha

N

Ft. Riley
■ Ft. Leavenworth
■ Ft. Hays

W ← → E

S

■ Ft. Reno
■ Ft. Cobb
■ Ft. Sill

0   500

Miles

■ Ft. Ringgold

Washington crossing the Delaware.

PREFACE

A number of significant military events have occurred during the Christmas season. George Washington's crossing of the Delaware River on the night of December 25, 1776, to attack unsuspecting Germans partaking in a little too much Christmas cheer became one of the most legendary events in history. Less known than Washington's holiday feat, the annual Christmas celebration at West Point in 1826 deteriorated into a mutinous "eggnog riot" involving more than a third of the corps of cadets. Following a decree that the holiday should be observed without alcohol, high-spirited Southern cadets (in particular) smuggled whiskey into the academy barracks and holiday festivities deteriorated into violence, including attempted murder. Cadet Jefferson Davis led the riot, while Cadet Robert E. Lee managed to remain aloof.

The Mexican War saw the sharp Christmas-day Battle of Bracito, which left sixty-three Mexicans dead. The victorious American troops, who suffered no deaths, celebrated Christmas night by throughly enjoying captured Mexican food, wine, and cigarillos. A generation later in 1864 General William Tecumseh Sherman sent a "Christmas card" in the form of a telegram to President Lincoln presenting the city of Savannah as a Christmas gift. The frontier army itself carried out several campaigns around the Christmas season, and the reality of bloodshed provided stark contrast to the usual joyous festivities. A dramatic example was the Indian survivors of the Wounded Knee Massacre, who were taken to a makeshift chapel hospital still decorated with Christmas finery.

As the army moved to foreign soil in more recent times, so did Christmastime conflicts. American-held Bastogne withstood a Christmas-day siege by the Germans in 1944. The Vietnam War had dragged on throughout many Christmases before President Nixon ordered the "Christmas bombing" of Hanoi and Haiphong in 1972, an effort which failed to produce victory. And you may recall Christmas 1992 and seeing the video of American soldiers bringing food to starving children in Somalia.

Clearly, Christmas is woven into the fabric of our military history. Nowhere was this history more charming, tragic, elegant, and memorable than in our own frontier army of 1865–1900. As you will see in *A Frontier Army Christmas*, these celebrations of Christmas were frequently dependent upon the whims of history and the fortunes of war.

Just as it took an entire garrison to put on a special frontier Christmas, so too is this volume the result of the contributions of many. We would like to thank the following staff members of the Nebraska State Historical Society for their support: Deb Brownson, Tom Buecker, John Carter, Dell Darling, Cindy Drake, Marty Miller, Cynthia Monroe, Eli Paul, Gail DeBuse Potter, Jim Potter, Marlene Roesler, Steve Ryan, and Linda Shanks.

Many individuals responded to our research requests or helped us in a variety of ways, including: Constance Wynn Altshuler, Tucson, Arizona; Elden Davis, Howell, Michigan; Susan Badger Doyle, Sheridan, Wyoming; Donna Dippie, Victoria, British Columbia; Nora Graf, Camp Verde, Arizona; Jerry Green, Fayetteville, Georgia; Jerome Greene, Denver, Colorado; Paul Hedren, Williston, North Dakota; Nancy Corbusier Knox, Santa Fe, New Mexico; Roye Lindsay, Burwell, Nebraska; Larry Ludwig, Fort Bowie, Arizona; Doug McChristian, Fort Laramie, Wyoming; William McKale, Fort Riley, Kansas; Tom Morrison, North Platte, Nebraska; Stephen Osman, St. Paul, Minnesota; Cecil Sanderson, Fort Bridger, Wyoming; Harold Schuler, Pierre, South Dakota; Towana Spivey, Fort Sill, Oklahoma; Patricia Stallard, Knoxville, Tennessee; Charles Trimble, Omaha, Nebraska; and Robert Wilhelm, Hays, Kansas.

We also appreciate the assistance of the staff from these institutions: American Heritage Center, University of Wyoming, Laramie, Wyoming; Beinecke Rare Book and Manuscript Library, Yale University, New Haven, Connecticut; Buffalo Bill Historical Center, Cody, Wyoming; Denver Public Library, Western History Collection, Denver, Colorado; Fort Abraham Lincoln State Historical Park, Mandan, North Dakota; Fort Huachuca Museum, Fort Huachuca, Arizona; Frederic Remington Art Museum, Ogdensburg, New York; Frontier Army Museum, Fort Leavenworth, Kansas; Historical Society of Douglas County, Omaha, Nebraska; Huntington Library, Art Collections, and Botanical Gardens, San Marino, California; Little Bighorn Battlefield National Monument, Crow Agency, Montana; Minnesota Historical Society, St. Paul, Minnesota; Museum of New Mexico, Santa Fe, New Mexico; National Archives, Washington, D.C.; New York State Historical Association Library, Cooperstown, New York; The Newberry Library, Chicago, Illinois; San Juan Island National Historical Park, Friday Harbor, Washington; South Dakota State Historical Society, Pierre, South Dakota; State Historical Society of North Dakota, Bismarck, North Dakota; United States Army Military Institute, Carlisle Barracks, Pennsylvania; United States Military Academy, West Point, New York; University of Kansas Libraries, Kansas Collection, Lawrence, Kansas; University of Pittsburgh Press, Pittsburgh, Pennsylvania; and the Wyoming State Archives, Wyoming Division of Cultural Resources, Cheyenne, Wyoming.

To one individual goes our special thanks, John D. McDermott, Sheridan, Wyoming. Jack generously opened his research files on this topic and provided us sources that we would have only obtained with great diffficulty.

We also wish to acknowledge the considerable moral support that our spouses provided during our project and who faithfully read each draft of our manuscript. Thank you Helen and Eli.

Finally, the inspiration for this book came from Dr. D. B. Wengert, who upon his return from the South Pacific during wartime improvised a Christmas. During a time of scarcity and rationing he made by hand an abundance of ornaments, many with a distinctive military theme, and gave his young son James a most memorable Christmas holiday.

INTRODUCTION

"Very different is the soldier's Christmas."

For the soldier stationed at a remote frontier post, Christmas celebrations were an important break in the otherwise monotonous routine of army life. For the soldier in the field, Christmas was merely another day on the calendar, usually spent fighting fatigue, dreadful weather, and sometimes Indians. Regardless of circumstances, these trailblazers left a marvelous array of remembrances of Christmases past in diaries, letters, and newspaper accounts that highlight their indefatigable spirit.

The way Christmas was celebrated in the frontier army depended as much upon location as anything else. Most posts on the northern plains were far from railroad lines and nearer to Indian agencies than large towns. Therefore, obtaining even the most basic goods was challenging. At those posts located on rail lines or near the West Coast, however, Christmas could be celebrated as fashionably as in the big, eastern cities. In addition, the presence of loved ones—women and children—at posts generally made for a merrier holiday.

For the women—arguably a civilizing influence—who lived at remote army posts, Christmas was one of the happiest times of the year. To paraphrase one book on the West, Christmas trees, like weddings and churchgoing, came West with women.[1] Fortunately many women did not take the advice of one anonymous soldier stationed at desolate Camp Arbuckle, Indian Territory, in 1852.

> **At this post we are denied all those delightfully pleasant church festivities common to all civilized and christian communities, for the simple reason that we have no Chaplain. Let all young ladies who are dazzled with the glare of gilt buttons at some of the fashionable parties on the East, bear these, and other deprivations, in mind, before saying "yes" to the fascinating sons of Mars.[2]**

Some of these "deprivations" were not eradicated ten or even twenty years after this man's friendly warning. Most army wives were not disheartened however. They relished making the holiday a festive time for all. When lacking even the most basic materials, these women called upon their creativity, ingenuity, and memory in fashioning decorations, preparing food, making gifts, and organizing entertainment.

For residents of frontier army posts, the celebration of Christmas was an exercise in imagination. Because of the difficulties they overcame to create a "traditional" Christmas, the holiday may have meant more to them. In some cases the desire to follow established customs resulted in elaborate, even ostentatious observances.

"The Corporal's Christmas Dinner." From *Harper's Weekly*, Dec. 17, 1892.

We present here an extensive sampling of frontier army Christmas celebrations as told through first person accounts. Geoffrey Williston Christine, a nineteenth-century journalist and astute observer, could just as easily have provided the introduction to this book. Many elements of a frontier army Christmas—the difficulties, the ingenuity, the enjoyment—appear in his short vignette, written in 1875.

> **Very different is the soldier's Christmas. Away out on the frontier, miles from any railroad, in a lonely little fort, surrounded by Indians, our army officers and their wives have no long rows of elegant shops from whose great supply of "holiday goods" they may select gifts for each other and their little ones as well as for the dear friends they have left behind them in their far eastern homes. They have no great array of market stalls loaded down with poultry, fruit and game, where they may purchase material for the Christmas dinner. For Christmas gifts and Christmas cheer they must depend entirely upon their own ingenuity. But what a wonderful genii that same ingenuity sometimes is, and what pretty things and pretty dishes he often evolves out of seemingly nothing, almost equaling in this respect the famous genii of Aladdin's wonderful lamp.**

In a little frontier post away out on the trackless plains of the far west where not a shrub or tree of any kind could be seen even beneath the scorching suns of summer, I have known quite a respectable Christmas tree to be "faked" by splicing together several walking sticks, fastening them upright through a hole in a soap box and covering them with green tissue paper obtained from the post store, where all sorts of odds and ends accumulate in the course of years. The branches were formed by winding the central portion of long, stiff pieces of heavy wire about the trunk, formed as above, and allowing their ends to project.

That same Christmas night we had a ball at the commandant's quarters, and everybody in garrison, including not a few Indians, gathered around our improvised Christmas tree which seemed to afford as much delight to the oldest person present as to the fairy-like little maiden of five years—the commandant's daughter and the idol of the fort—for whom it had been fabricated.[3]

As scholars of the frontier army are well aware, the histories of forts, campaigns, and generals give short shrift to this subject. Not everyone who served in the frontier army observed Christmas, and the holiday is not a topic usually found in the index of the typical western historical work. When one looks to the first person accounts of frontier army life, though, the importance of this holiday readily becomes apparent. If celebrating Christmas made little, if any, contribution to the "Winning of the West," it provided a boost to morale and a needed connection to a more peaceful time and a more settled place.

While we have tried to confine our story to the 1865–1900 period, we have extended those dates to accommodate a few of the most compelling accounts and illustrations. Divided into ten chapters, *A Frontier Army Christmas* offers a series of contrasting images of Christmas: war and peace, officers and enlisted soldiers, men and women, adults and children. Compare, if you will, Elizabeth Custer's enthusiasm for Christmas celebrations with Caroline Frey Winne's utter lack of it. Each of these women, both officers' wives, dealt with the hardships of army life in their own way. Mrs. Winne is herself a paradox, finally coming around in later years, conquering her homesickness, and celebrating Christmas wholeheartedly. Notice the Christmases of Lt. John G. Bourke, who one year is practically freezing to death on a campaign to find Crazy Horse and in another is displaying his collection of Indian bric-a-brac for the Omaha elite.

We consider this valuable source material for historic site and museum curators, reenactors, aficionados of western lore, those fascinated by life and manners of the Victorian period, and those interested in the broader topic of the history and traditions of Christmas. These are clearly nineteenth century accounts, though, and reflect the times and prejudices of the authors. No attempt has been made to sanitize their words.

Finding these accounts and presenting them anew have been challenging but pleasurable tasks. We sincerely hope you not only will enjoy reading them but will search out other dusty gems in the diaries, letters, and newspapers of your locale or favorite fort. Enjoy! And the merriest of an old army Christmas to you.

Notes

[1] Joan Reiter, *The Old West: The Women* (Alexandria, Va.: Time-Life Books, 1978), 40.

[2] John E. Baur, *Christmas on the American Frontier, 1800-1900* (Caldwell, Ida.: The Caxton Printers, Ltd., 1961), 232.

[3] *Omaha Daily Bee,* undated clipping from the files of the Historical Society of Douglas County, Omaha.

Chapter One

CHRISTMAS IN GARRISON

"Christmas in Garrison is celebrated by all the demonstrations of joy and good cheer."

Life at a frontier army post was often dreary, sometimes frightening, always governed by rules, regulations, and etiquette. However, these posts could also be the setting of great scenes of happiness, friendship, and joy. The celebration of Christmas was one of the times when the garrison's monotonous routine could be broken.

In 1886 an anonymous army wife submitted a letter to the editor of the *Army and Navy Register,* issuing the following challenge to those in the frontier army.

The monotony of the Army on the frontier, both for officers and men, is its crying evil. Especially is this true of the five years' enlistment of a soldier. The same monotonous drill, the same routine, without even a change of diet. With nothing to look forward to but the (doubtful) pleasure of the target season and a possible practice march, and for dissipation and excitement an occasional drunk, what wonder that young men grow restless and desert? "All work and no play makes Jack a dull boy."

It is plainly the duty of commanding officers and company commanders to vary the monotony by encouraging and proposing amusements for enlisted men. And as the never-old festival of brotherly love approaches we should think of these men, far from home and kindred, and have some festival in which rich and poor, rank and file alike, could join, something on the old plantation style before the war. If the soldiers among themselves have any histrionic ability, a bright and witty play would enliven their Christmas very much. If not, the officers and ladies can easily get up tableaux among themselves to be given Christmas eve or Christmas night, for the children and adults as well.

If among the officers' and laundresses' families there are many children, a Christmas tree will be found to be most acceptable. Pains should be taken that not a single child in the garrison is left out. The expense will be found to be trifling if each officer's child contributes some toy from its superabundant stock, to be hung upon the tree for its less fortunate neighbor. Thus the pleasure of giving will be incul-

cated early. If none of these entertainments are possible, a magic lantern show, or even a concert, is better than no festivity. Of course, each and every one of these entertainments should be given in the public hall of the post and every soldier made welcome.

I hope these suggestions may help to vary the dullness of at least one of the posts this winter.[1]

An anonymous soldier's wife at Fort Yates, North Dakota, was one of those who responded to the 1886 summons.

The suggestions made in the *Army and Navy Register* by "An Officer's Wife" some weeks since was carried out at this post. Thursday evening a beautiful Christmas tree greeted the children of the post in the "hop room." Every child in the garrison, officers', soldiers', laundresses', civilian employees' little ones were all there and each and every one found a toy, an apple, an orange, a bag of candy and popcorn "galore." Santa Claus appeared and appointed Major Brown and Lieutenant Barth, Twelfth Infantry, to distribute the gifts.

The credit of this happy time must be given to the Misses Wood—Miss Maggie, Miss May and Miss Sallie—who originated the plan, collected the money, every officer cheerfully "chipped in" when assailed by such fair beggars, and ordered the toys, etc., while all the ladies of the post assisted in preparing the tree, and everybody was there to see the fun, and a happier set of little ones never gathered together.[2]

Perhaps these army wives did not realize that for two decades before the 1886 challenge and response, residents of frontier army posts, in one way or another, enjoyed as elaborate a Christmas celebration as they could muster.

Company B, Second Cavalry, hosted a ball for Christmas 1866, as described in a letter from Cottonwood Springs (Fort McPherson), Nebraska, to the editor of the *Omaha Daily Herald*.

In order that the inhabitants of the civilized world may see that, though we are amongst the Buffaloes and the Indians, we can still enjoy the amusements of the States, the following sketch may not prove uninteresting to the numerous circle of your readers.

Company "B" 2nd United States Cavalry upon the evening of December 25th gave a ball to the inhabitants of Cottonwood and its suburbs. It was well attended and by the smiling faces of the guests and the number of smiles taken in the refreshment room, every one seemed to enjoy themselves.

Fort Cottonwood (later Fort McPherson), Nebraska Territory, 1864. Courtesy Joslyn Art Museum.

The supper was gotten up under the able supervision of one of the members of the Company, and would do credit even to Monsieur Soyer himself. After mature discussion, the Gourmands that partook thereof, unanimously pronounced it excellent.

The decorations were extremely elegant and tasteful, and the floor in good order and comfortable to dance upon. The votaries of Tepsichorra going through the ways of the giddy dance without any mishaps.

The soldiers behaved, as soldiers should, like gentlemen, and not one word or action was heard or seen to disturb the equanimity that prevailed during the whole evening.

The officers of the garrison were present and were noticeable for their urbanity toward private soldiers. Having been a soldier myself, I can appreciate (as any one can that has served in the ranks) any condescension on the part of the officers, and the manner in which the officers behaved upon the night of the ball reflects great credit upon themselves, tends to make the soldier esteem his officers more and heightens the respect he ought to feel for his superiors.[3]

Ada A. Vogdes, wife of Lt. Anthony W. Vogdes, Fourth Infantry, rhapsodized on her 1869 Christmas at Fort Fetterman, Wyoming.

Christmas at Fetterman. A brighter or more glorious day never dawned in the south of France than the one now passed: a clear blue sky with a soft haziness in the air equalled only by a June day. The ground, however covered with snow, did not seem in the least to affect the air.

In the evening Col. Wilson, the sutler, gave us a delightful party, the first I believe ever given here, and we had a nice time even though there were only two ladies present. We had two violins and a number of delightful gentlemen dancers. The supper, which was announced at eleven, was delicious: jellies, cakes of all kinds, chicken salad, roasted rabbit, tongue, sardines, raisins, almonds, candy, and the most delicious cooked chicken I ever ate, to say nothing of the cream, coffee and wines. After tea we only stayed a little while, as it was Sunday morning and too late for Christians to stay longer. The rooms were beautifully decorated with flags and evergreens and looking glasses.[4]

A correspondent to the *Cheyenne Daily Leader* reported that Fort Laramie, Wyoming, celebrated Christmas 1875 with much enthusiasm.

Good old Christmas was fitly celebrated in Fort Laramie. On Christmas Eve the old Fort, that has withstood so many "bloody" sieges, presented an appearance really magnificent. Co. K, 3rd Cavalry, being the only company in the post, displayed their usual energy (for which they are deservedly noted, both in field and camp), in making the past Christmas a merry one at the old Fort. Every window in the post was brilliantly illuminated with a dozen candles each, the quarters were decorated with evergreen, and in the old band quarters were as merry a set of dancers as ever tripped the "light fantastic toe." All went merry as a marriage bell. Wine flowed freely, and many a hearty toast was drank [sic] to the happiness of old friends in Cheyenne.[5]

Fanny Corbusier wanted Christmas 1877 to be a special one for her husband, army surgeon William H. Corbusier ("father"). Holiday preparations at their Camp Sheridan, Nebraska, quarters kept the family busy and served as a warm homecoming for Surgeon Corbusier after his two-week absence.

One Christmas Eve, as father had been gone nearly two weeks, we expected him home and worked fast to have everything ready for the commemoration before he arrived. Capt. [Emmett] Crawford and the boys strung cranberries; Louie and I made mince pie, fruit cakes, crullers, and other good things. The pine tree, which the captain had brought down from the hills the day before, was brought in and pine branches hung on the walls.

The weather was very cold, and as the sun sank westward, it grew bitterly so. I began to fear that father would not come—

Army surgeon William H. Corbusier, 1875. NSHS-P853.

half hoping that he was not out in the cold—but shortly after sunset he arrived. Both he and the driver had to run alongside of the ambulance nearly half way, to keep them from freezing, the intense cold having descended suddenly after they left the agency.

After the boys had gone to bed, we decorated the tree, with Capt. Crawford as much in sympathy with the occasion as if he were with his own family. Our Christmas Day and dinner were all that could be desired. We had sent a wagon to the railroad, 162 miles, as we did about once a month, for supplies that we had ordered at Grand Isle [Island], Neb. There, many articles were quite reasonable—eggs, 10c a dozen—butter, 15c a pound—chickens 10c a pound—turkeys and ducks, 12c. We sent to Chicago for Booth's oysters which came in flat tin cans, packed in ice, so that the dinner we sat down to was a sumptuous one. After our repast we all went over to the barracks with Capt. Crawford to inspect the men's dinner. The boys liked these "inspections" as they were always treated to plum duff, which they pronounced a delicious dish.[6]

Fort Pembina, located in extreme northern Dakota Territory, celebrated Christmas 1878 with as much fervor as any small town would have mustered.

Christmas was indeed a holiday at this post and vicinity, and the following will probably give your readers an idea of how it was spent in part of the Red river country.

The children who attend school at Pembina gave a festival Christmas eve at Brown's Hall. Music, recitations, dialogues and tableaux vivants constituted the programme. Every one of the young ones performed their parts in a creditable manner. Where all done well, it is difficult to make any distinction, but the audience seemed to be partial and most pleased with the efforts of the Misses Collins and Cavalier and the brothers of the two mentioned young ladies, and they were deserving of the many rounds of applause which greeted their efforts.

The entertainment was gotten up by the village school-master, to whose efforts much of its success may be attributed, and was greatly enjoyed by all who attended.

At the fort, the Christmas dinner was the all-absorbing topic of the day, and such a dinner I have never even seen before in the army. Company K's dinner was a Christmas gift from its captain, Thos. G. Troxel, and I don't think could or has been ever surpassed for elegance, costliness and splendor. Oysters in every imaginable style, stuffed turkeys, geese, roasted meats, hams, a half-dozen different kind[s] of vegetables, together with the many kinds of pie, cake, candy, fruit and beverages, comprised a lot of dainties and solid food, which but very seldom appears on the regular bill of fare of a soldier's mess.

The dining-room had been tastefully decorated. Emblems and devices representing the various branches of the service adorned the walls, and mottoes of every description in silver and gold, surrounded with evergreens and artificial flowers, made a very pleasant sight to behold. Over the door leading to the dining-room were the words "Welcome," and underneath "Company K, Seventeenth United States Infantry," elaborately gotten up and highly ornamented.

The table fairly groaned under its load of the good things of life, and was really a magnificent sight. At 1 o'clock p.m., the dinner-bell sounded, and our officers welcomed us to the festive board. Our excellent and worthy captain made a few remarks appropriate to the occasion, to which Sergeant M. L. Russell on behalf of the company responded. Then the boys attacked the eatables, and the way they disappeared would lead one to think that none of them had had anything to eat for a month.

In fact, I believe myself that the majority fasted for three days, or longer, in order to be able to enjoy their Christmas dinner.

During the evening the Fort Pembina Glee Club and String Band serenaded its officers, and a pleasant hour was thus spent. The men's efforts to please were duly appreciated, and their various songs and music elicited loud and frequent applause.[7]

Presumably every fort had its share of "Scrooges." For some, simple dinner parties did not fulfill their idea of what Christmas festivities should include. For others, the desolation of the frontier led to loneliness. Inclement weather also played a role in "bah-humbug" sentiments.

Col. Philippe Regis de Trobriand, a French emigre and commander of Fort Stevenson, Dakota Territory, in 1867 wrote of a rather cheerless holiday.

Christmas Eve! No Christmas supper for us. Everyone stays in his hut, probably dreaming of past memories that this date recalls. Outside, after a stormy day, the night is clear; the stars twinkle. Inside, the lonely lamp burns until the customary hour of retiring. Nothing marks this night from all the others, and if the calendar did not indicate that today is the twenty-fourth of December, no sign in heaven or on earth would reveal to us here that tonight the Christian world is festive, and that in families everywhere, the children, little and big, are rejoicing around the Christmas tree! And midnight mass! And the religious hymn of Victor Adam:

> *Minuit, chretiens, c'est l'heure solennelle*
> *Ou l'Homme-Dieu descendit jusqu' a nous. . .*

Thursday, December 26. Finally, finally, I have moved into my log house. Yesterday, Christmas, passed like the others in my cabin, except that in the evening I dined with Mr. and Mrs. Marshal. Lieutenants Norwell and Ellis were in the party. Food plentiful, conversation banal and uninteresting. I finished the evening with Dr. and Mrs. Gray who had Major Furey and Lieutenant Hooton to dinner.[8]

Col. Philippe Regis de Trobriand painted this 1867–68 winter scene of Fort Stevenson, Dakota Territory. Courtesy State Historical Society of North Dakota.

For those who could not celebrate the holiday in the style to which they were accustomed, Christmas often passed as just another day on the calendar. Caroline Frey Winne, a New Yorker who once said she would not live in Nebraska for all the wealth in the state, was unhappy about celebrating the holiday in the West. Married to Charles K. Winne, post surgeon at Sidney Barracks, she communicated dourly to her brother of Christmas 1876.

> **We have closed our second year at this post. Tomorrow will be the third New Year's day. It hasn't seemed at all like holiday week. Christmas was quiet—as every other day—and very cold, as the whole week has been. Tomorrow we are invited out to dine at the R.R. House. The gentleman who owns & keeps this house with his family are about the nicest people we have met since we came out here. . . .**
>
> **An invitation to dinner, or in fact any invitation & outside the post too, is a wonderful thing to us. We, no doubt, will have a good dinner, and it is a pleasure to spend a few hours with people who are congenial—and that the most of Army people are not.[9]**

Pvt. Wilmot P. Sanford, Co. D, Sixth Infantry, recorded his 1876 Christmas at Fort Buford, North Dakota. There is certainly nothing very merry about his holiday, all too common for the enlisted man.

> **Sunday December 24, 1876. Clear and cold. 16 weeks more. Excused from Inspectin. Co Inspectin in blouses by the Captain. On guard No 1 of the 2nd relief. Liet Rivers officer of the day. Scott, Sar Robinsin, Cop. Prisiners out to werk all day. 6 prisiners. Some of the men on a drunk already. Duff for dinner and supper. Cold night. 22 below zero in the night. Wind changable, but windy. Most East.**
>
> **Monday December 25, 1876. Clear and cold 28 below. Came off guard in the morning and to the quarters the rest of the day. Having a good drink. Corn, Peaches, jelly, butter, duff and roast beef and gravy and whiskey drinks. 3 galons to the Co by the sutlers. Howard ordly [orderly] today. Half the Co were drunk before night. No werk today. Took a sleep in the afternoon. Gave Sar his watch. Men going down a little for the storm. Wind North.[10]**

Some celebrants harped on what had not been received in time for Christmas. Poor mail delivery produced disappointments. Marion T. Brown, a visitor to Fort Sill in 1886, expressed her dismay at not receiving a much-anticipated package and Christmas cards in a letter to her mother.

>   Your letter of the 21st came on the 24th but the package
> containing the Christmas cards and Carrie's fan has not
> appeared. We were very much disappointed about the cards
> for Dr. Taylor on Christmas eve and more so in the morning
> when his man came over bringing each of us a present from
> him. Mrs. S's was a large bottle of nice perfume and a pretty
> riding whip for each of us girls. If the cards ever get here,
> there will be no pleasure in presenting them, for it will look
> as though we sent for them as an after thought. C. has written
> Mr. S. over and over that it took a package seven or eight days
> to get here, so there is no excuse for his being so slow.
>   . . .Yesterday all of the officers and ladies went to "inspect"
> the Christmas dinners in the soldiers quarters and at the
> hospital. We were invited to go and of course went. They had
> elegant dinners. Turkey etc. etc.
>   . . .Maybe I was a little cross about the Christmas cards, but
> we were so disappointed.[11]

Perhaps Marion Brown should have adopted the attitude of Elizabeth Custer, wife of the Seventh Cavalry's ill-fated George Armstrong Custer. She threw herself wholeheartedly into the Christmas holidays, and it may not be too much of an exaggeration to say that Libby Custer enjoyed Christmas more than any other person in the frontier army.

>   Sometimes I think our Christmas on the frontier was a
> greater event to us than to any one in the states. We all had to
> do so much to make it a success.
>   One universal custom was for all of us to spend all the time
> we could together. All day long the officers were running in
> and out of every door, the "wish you Merry Christmas" rang
> out over the parade ground after any man who was crossing
> to attend to some duty and had not shown up among us. We
> usually had a sleigh ride and everyone sang and laughed as we
> sped over the country where there were no neighbors to be
> disturbed by our gaiety. If it was warm enough there poured
> out of garrison a cavalcade vehemently talking, gesticulating,
> laughing or humming bars of Christmas carols remembered
> from childhood, or starting some wild or convivial chorus
> where everybody announced that they "wouldn't go home till
> morning" in notes very emphatic if not entirely musical.
>   The feast of the day over, we adjourned from dinner to play
> some games of our childhood in order to make the states and
> our homes seem a little nearer. Later in the evening, when the
> music came up from the band quarters, we all went to the
> house of the commanding officer to dance.

With a garrison full of perfectly healthful people with a determination to be merry, notwithstanding the isolated life and útterly dreary surroundings, the holidays were made something to look forward to the whole year round.[12]

Elizabeth and George Custer (center row), **Fort Abraham Lincoln.**
Courtesy Little Bighorn Battlefield National Monument.

Notes

[1] *Army and Navy Register* (hereafter cited as *ANR*), Nov. 10, 1886.

[2] Ibid., Jan. 12, 1887.

[3] "How the Soldiers Celebrated Christmas at Cottonwood," *Omaha Daily Herald*, Jan. 12, 1867.

[4] Donald K. Adams, ed., "The Journal of Ada A. Vodges, 1868-71," *Montana The Magazine of Western History* 13 (July 1963):9-10.

[5] *Cheyenne Daily Leader*, Jan. 19, 1876.

[6] William T. Corbusier, *Verde to San Carlos, Recollections of a Famous Army Surgeon and His Observant Family on the Western Frontier, 1869-1886* (Tucson: Dale Stuart King, 1969), 164-66.

[7] *St. Paul Pioneer-Press*, Jan. 2, 1879.

[8] Lucile M. Kane, ed., *Military Life in Dakota: The Journal of Philippe Regis de Trobriand* (St. Paul, Minn.: Alvord Memorial Commission, 1951), 194-95.

[9] Thomas R. Buecker, ed., "Letters of Caroline Frey Winne from Sidney Barracks and Fort McPherson, Nebraska, 1874-1878," *Nebraska History* 62 (Spring 1981):27.

[10] Michael D. Hill and Ben Innis, ed., "The Fort Buford Diary of Private Sanford, 1876-1877," *North Dakota History* 52 (Summer 1985):32.

[11] C. Richard King, ed., *Marion T. Brown: Letters From Fort Sill, 1886-1887* (Austin: The Encino Press, 1970), 37-38.

[12] Walter F. Peterson, ed., "Christmas on the Plains," *The American West* 1 (Fall 1964):54,57.

Capt. Augustus Whittemore Corliss, Eighth Infantry, left a long record in his personal diary of Christmases in several garrisons where he was stationed during the 1880s. Regardless of his post, Corliss made every effort to celebrate the season well for his children's sake.

Fort Halleck, Nevada

Tuesday, Dec. 23, 1884

Cold and windy. At work all day on the Christmas tree for the little ones.

Wednesday, Dec. 24, 1884

A cold, rainy day. Worked most of the day for the children's christmas tree, and at 5 P.M. their hearts were made glad by a sight of the pretty tree and its load of toys, &c. &c. many of which have come from far-off friends. I got as a Christmas present from my wife a large and beautiful meerschaum pipe with the crossed rifles and number of my regiment and my initials cut on the front.

Thursday, Dec. 25, 1884

Cool and fine. Spent most of the day explaining the new toys to Bob and Cricket. Mr. & Mrs. D.T. Alger dined with us, and in the evening Lieut. Summerhayes and wife, Chas. E. Mayer and wife and Lieut. Geo. W. Ruthers came in and we played "keno" and had a late supper.

Angel Island, California

Monday, Dec. 21, 1885

A very rainy forenoon. Wife went to town to buy Christmas things. On duty as officer of the day.

Tuesday, Dec. 22, 1885

A rainy day. Went to town shopping.... Returned to the post in evening. . . .

Wednesday, Dec. 23, 1885

A raw, rainy day. Went to town in the forenoon. . .to attend to business for which I was called by a telegram, and returned to the post in the evening. Busy with a Christmas tree for the children.

Thursday, Dec. 24, 1885

A very rainy afternoon. Busy all day with the Christmas tree, to which, in the evening, all the children in the post flocked. Afterwards we all went to see the tree of General Kautz. Of course our children are wild over all the new toys.

Friday, Dec. 25, 1885

Cold and raw, with heavy rain in evening. Lieut. George W. Ruthers and Miss Minnie Scott dined with us.

Fort Robinson, Nebraska

Thursday, Dec. 23, 1886

A cold day. At home all day, reading. Maj. Burt's family, wife, daughter, and son arrived at the post.

Friday, Dec. 24, 1886

Cold day. My wife returned from Fremont. At home all day.

Saturday, Dec. 25, 1886

Cold and windy. Bob and Cricket happy over their new toys. At home all day.

Fort Robinson, Nebraska

Monday, Dec. 19, 1887

A bitter cold windy day, with some snow. At home all day. Busy with preparations for Christmas.

Tuesday, Dec. 20, 1887

Cold and very windy. Mercury at four below zero at 7 A.M., and not above zero all day. At home, writing.

Wednesday, Dec. 21, 1887

A cold, windy day. At home all day, reading.

Thursday, Dec. 22, 1887

A cold, windy day, with a little snow. Went to Crawford and back in afternoon with Capt. Hughes and Mrs. Bailey after Christmas toys.

Friday, Dec. 23, 1887

Fine day. Busy all day with the Christmas tree for the children.

Saturday, Dec. 24, 1887

Cool and pleasant. At home all day. In the evening we had our Christmas tree, at which gathered all the children up and down the officers' line, each one having a present of some kind. Bob and Cricket, being general favorites, had many presents. I gave my wife a silver-plated soup tureen, a carver & fork, &c. I got "Hawley's Operations of War," a standard English book.

Sunday, Dec. 25, 1887

Fine day. Light fall of snow in the evening. At home most of the day, reading and writing. First Sergeant Emanuel Stance, Troop "F," 9th Cavalry, was murdered between the post and Crawford in the evening, probably by men of his own troop.

Monday, Dec. 26, 1887

A cold, blustering day, with light fall of snow. In the evening a Christmas tree was lighted for the post children in the amusement hall.

Tuesday, Dec. 27, 1887

Very cold day. Mercury at 26° below zero at 7:30 A.M. At 8 P.M. it was 6° below. No clue yet to murderers of Sergeant Stance, but some men are suspected.

Fort Robinson, Nebraska

Saturday, Dec. 22, 1888

Fine and warm. At home all day. Benj. S. Paddock, post trader, went to Omaha.

Sunday, Dec. 23, 1888

Cold and cloudy. At home all day, reading.

Monday, Dec. 24, 1888

Cold, with light fall of snow. The children both happy in the possession of a quantity of presents of various kinds.

Tuesday, Dec. 25, 1888

A cold, windy day. About three inches of snow on the ground. Bob on the ice with skates for the first time. Dr. G. W. Adair and Lieut. Richard H. Wilson dined with us today.

Fort Robinson, Nebraska

Tuesday, Dec. 24, 1889

Cool and fine. In the evening a grand Christmas tree for all the children in the garrison was held at the amusement hall.

Wednesday, Dec. 25, 1889

A vile, dusty day. Spent the most of the day at home. Lieut Frank Owen dined with us.

Augustus Whittemore Corliss Diaries, 1884–1898, Denver Public Library.

Chapter Two

IN THE FIELD

"Left camp as yousel and spent my Crismas on the road."

Winter campaigning was never enjoyable, and, as the calendar drew near the Christmas season, many soldiers detailed their hardships and their longing for home. The threat of possible battle was always present regardless of the date, as Winfield Scott Haney wrote in his diary. Haney, a troop blacksmith for Custer's Seventh Cavalry, also missed the traditional Christmas feast.

> **Near Fort Cobb, Ind. Ter. Dec. 24, 1868. Reveille at day break. The morning is very pleasant. I went for wood and found plenty of it where I was. We had a scare last evening about nine o'clock. The whole regiment came out under arms, but it was only a false alarm and nobody was hurt. No treaty yet but we expect the Indians all in soon.**
>
> **Dec. 25, 1868. The morning is cool and windy and very dusty. Today is Christmas Day and I have only two hard tacks for my dinner and a quart of bean soup that a hog would not eat if he were starving. This is the kind of a dinner I have to sit down today, alright. Everything is lovely.[1]**

Sgt. Herman Werner's recollection of Christmas 1884 campaigning in the mountains of Montana with Troop L, First Cavalry, is literate but not romantic.

> **Daylight of another day crept slowly into this basin. It was Christmas eve, the day before Christmas. Our honored captain decreed it to be the day for rest and all of us felt better. Christmas eve of 1884 found us not in the Holy Land. The Bethlehem for Troop L, First Cavalry, in the year of 1884 was within the fastness of the Little Rocky Mountains, Montana, on a day when a temperature of forty-two below zero painfully penetrated to the very marrow of man and beast.[2]**

The story continues as Werner and his fellow soldiers searched for a supposed band of fifty or more renegades. They did not find the Indians, but they did find a herd of cattle, one of which became their dinner.

> **We loaded our horses with two hind-quarters, the neck and chunks from the ribs, and with that we returned to unloaded [sic] our horses—by this time, frozen chunks of fresh beef—a**

real treat for a Christmas eve dinner, which was further enriched by frozen hardtacks and black coffee.

Our second night at this hollow passed noisy enough. Again the pack of hungry wolves were wide-awake. The odors of boiling fresh meat made the pack bolder. The sentries guarding our horses found it necessary to fire into the pack on several occasions during the night. A dozen or so large owls that roosted nearby seemed to hoot louder, and as if for our special benefit they chorused a doleful Christmas eve song into the midnight hours. And the winds again sounded noisily. It was at an early hour when we broke camp. It was Christmas morning.

It was not the bells from the belfry of a Christian cathedral that we heard. Instead, it was the bell that hung around the neck of a pack mule, around the neck of the boss mule, the leader of our pack animals. This now shaggy looking beast, and if to ridicule our fervent thought, shook its neck that carried the signal bell more often, and more violent than on any former days.[3]

John G. Bourke, about 1882.
NSHS-B774-1.

Lt. John G. Bourke, Third Cavalry, campaigning with Crook in the Superstition Mountains, Arizona, made a brief but poignant mention of the 1872 holiday in his diary.

Xmas comes but once a year. The day opened bright and genial just such a one as I hope our folks at home are having with the addition of good cheer, which we have not. Rations beginning to shorten. Broke camp at 8:45 a.m.[4]

The cold weather and boredom of the Washita Campaign in 1868 led David L. Spotts and his comrades, members of the Nineteenth Kansas Volunteer Cavalry and far from the fighting, to invent a way of staying warm.

Wednesday, December 23, 1868

There is not much doing in camp today and the boys in the company are hatching up an idea to create some excitement. Our great want is more room in our tent, so we conclude to dig a square hole, the size of our tent, deep enough so we can stand.

On one side we dig the floor six or eight inches deeper and make our bed on the higher portion. Tomorrow we will make a fireplace in the side where the floor is low and then we can sit on our bed before the fire.

We will not have to hunt so much wood nor have such a big fire to keep warm. Nearly all the company have begun making dugouts, or will do so. It is a great protection from the weather and much more comfortable. We have an arrangement that one of us is on duty each night, so we have fire all night and also have more room in our tent.

Thursday, December 24, 1868

Our fireplace is a good idea so we spend much of our time inside lying on our beds. We cook our meals inside now and use a wide box lid for a table. Many of the company boys have been to see our new home and have the "idea." Many of them are hard at it and will soon be comfortable. Our chimney draws nicely and we are not troubled with smoke. While out grazing our horses today we pulled enough dead grass to make a much softer bed than the one we had last night.

Our fire makes enough light that we could read if we had anything to read, so one of the boys in the squad got a deck of cards somewhere and we borrowed them and play once in a while. I do not know any of the games except euchre but Ingleman is a pretty good player and knows several games. One is what he calls seven-up—also cribbage. I think I will like the last game, but he says it requires a counter, but he will make one and then I can learn it.

This is Christmas Eve and we lie on our bed and tell what we would likely be doing if we were at home. I told them I would very likely be at some church's Christmas tree and have a good time.

Friday, December 25, 1868

Merry Christmas! It is a very cold day and it is my turn to stand guard. The wind is blowing a hurricane from the north and we have the sides up around the big tent so it is a protection to our dog tent which is about twenty feet south. Several of the tents in my company have been torn loose by the wind and the boys are pounding stakes to make them more secure. It so happens we have very little provisions in the commissary and I can get inside and on top of a pile of boxes where I can see everywhere inside, so I asked Sergt. Mather if I can sit up there and watch things. He told me "All right," so I am

protected from the wind and is so much more comfortable, besides it requires only one man and we do not get so cold.

We surely enjoy sitting by our fireplace today. When I am off duty I write letters to my home folks and to some of my schoolmates. Sergt. Mather came in today to see how we were and was very much pleased that we were so comfortable. Sergt. Casebier has not "lived" with us, but goes to his company except to relieve us. The other boys have three tents and are fixed nearly as well as we are, only one has a fireplace yet.[5]

Celebrating the season among cacti instead of evergreens while campaigning in the southwest, while no doubt warmer, did not ease a soldier's homesickness. Corp. E. A. Bode, Company D, Sixteenth Infantry Regiment, wrote of a Christmas in the field near Fort Concho, Texas, in 1880.

It was Christmas as we crossed a plain of cactus and sage, and occasionally a mesquite tree, while here and there a pretty prairie flower would repay us with its beautiful color.

A guarded spring at the head of one of the numerous valleys made our home for one night. We lay that evening under the bright rays of luna, thinking of the happy days of boyhood when standing around a decorated Christmas tree admiring our presents. We [thought] of a poor wretch from the ranks of the colored troops stationed to guard the spring who had been killed by one of his comrades and buried that afternoon a short distance from camp with all the military honors due a soldier, but over whose grave the wolves were howling.[6]

Lt. John Bigelow's attempts to share the 1885 holiday with some locals, while in the field in Arizona with the Tenth Cavalry, did little to ease his own loneliness.

I was visited this afternoon by my Mexican neighbors, man, woman, and two children. I took them to see the pig unearthed and treated them in my tent to cigarettes and canned peaches. The latter were enjoyed especially by the children. The little boy having eaten all I gave him, which was more, I thought, than was good for him, helped his sister finish hers.

Like myself, these good people spent their Christmas eve at home. It was a more cheerless evening than the ordinary one to me, a howling wind flapping my loose canvas, and making my candle flicker, so that I could hardly read. The illumination of my tent consists of two stearine candles stuck through a hole in the top of an [sic] yeast powder can filled with sand to give it stability.[7]

After a lengthy campaign in late 1874, Thompson McFadden, a civilian scout during Nelson Miles's Red River War, cleverly presented himself as a Christmas gift to his wife.

> **December 25th: I am now only twenty-five miles from home so I lose no time in hiring a conveyance and at noon I have the extreme pleasure of presenting myself to my better half as a Christmas gift and she was well pleased with the offering, as five months of service [which] is in the nature of it liable to make a widow at any time, seems a long time to the one waiting.[8]**

Contract Surgeon Henry R. Porter, in the field near Camp Verde, Arizona, in 1872, wrote a touching letter home to his father. It revealed his fondness for the traditional home cooked holiday meal, especially when no similar delicacies were available.

> **I will close by wishing you all a Merry Xmas and Happy New Year. I should like to be there and eat one of Mother's famous apple dumplings or plum puddings but I shall be obliged to content myself eating my Christmas dinner on the ground and made up of whatever we can get.[9]**

Maj. George W. Schofield, Tenth Cavalry, in the field near Fort Sill, Indian Territory, enjoyed a brief respite from the action. The amusement for the Christmas holiday in 1874 provided good target practice for future operations.

> **Dec. 25th. Sent a detachment with one Indian Scout as guide, and two days rations, eastward toward the Cheyenne Agency in the hope of hearing from Captain Keyes, and to scout that section of the country, marched the column across East Barry's Creek to, and down a fork of Deer Creek. Went into camp at 12:30 P.M. Had a contest between the three companies present, by three picked men from each, at target firing for a Christmas Turkey. Just before dark the detachment and Indian sent out in the morning to be gone two days, came into camp.**
>
> **They reported having seen one Cheyenne, that they had followed him for a short distance and then lost sight of him, that they soon after heard the firing from toward where the command was supposed to be, and thinking that fight was going on had hurried in. It being nearly dark no attempt was made to ascertain whether or not their story about the hostile Indian was true.[10]**

The winter Powder River Campaign followed the disastrous summer of 1876, when George Custer's Seventh Cavalry was defeated at the Little Bighorn. This Christmastime expedition boasts extensive documentation. The command found itself near Pumpkin Buttes, Wyoming, in 1876. Here the soldiers looked for Crazy Horse and tried to stay warm. We are fortunate to have reminiscences of this bitterly cold operation from the viewpoint of enlisted men, noncoms, and officers. Pvt. William Earl Smith recounted the terrible cold in which the soldiers suffered.

Sunday Dec. 24th 1876

Well morning came at last yes at last and I was never as glad to see a morning in all my life for such a nite as I had poot in. I had to keep awake to keep from freezing to death. Corpral [David] Hall was in charge of the gard and I can all ways see him sitting by that sage Brush fire a bout as big as a wash pan with five blankets raped [wrapped] around him. When I

Frederic Remington's painting, "Captain Baldwin Hunting the Hostile Camp," depicted the harsh conditions that faced the frontier soldier on a winter **campaign.** Courtesy Frederic Remington Art Museum, Ogdensburg, New York.

"General Crook's Head-quarters, Fort Fetterman," *Harper's Weekly*, Dec. 17, 1876.

walked my two ours [hours] I run all the time and a round and a round I went and never stoped till my time was up. I was now pooty warm and thought I could sleep. I lade down with 14 Blankets over me and a lot under me but it would not work for I frose out and had to git out and pool [pull] Sage Bruch and run a round.

We left camp as yousel and made 12 mils and camped on Sage crick and there was no wood hear neather but I had a stove in the tent and I and my Bunkey Pooled Sage Brush a nuff to keep warm with. This nite the thormometer was frose up and they could not tell how cold it was [but it was] the same the nite before this Nite. I went over to the commeiceres [commissary] and bought one can of Peaches. I gave 2 dollars for a can. I saw one man give 10 dollars for a bottle of Whiskey. I eate the Peaches. Crismas love. My bunkey helped.

Monday Dec. 25th 1876
Left camp as yousel and spent my Crismas on the road. Walked nearley all day. Made 20 mils and camped on some wotter holls. no wood. We had a reglar Old Crismas Dinner. A little peace of fat bacon and hard tack and a half a cup of coffee. You bet I thought of home now if ever I did. But fate was a gane me and I could not bee there. My Bunkey bought some candy and we ate it.[11]

First Sgt. James S. McClellan, Company H, Third Cavalry, recalled the tortuous cold without even a mention of holiday festivities.

> **Dec. 22 '76 Broke camp at 6 AM and marched up river 10 miles. I had on a hat and suffered greatly from cold as it snowed all day.**
>
> **Dec. 23 Marched up river and went in to camp late. made only about 15 miles it was extremely cold to-day and a strong wind. There was a lot of men frozen and during the night 2 mules died from cold.**
>
> **Dec. 24 Marched 8 miles up river and camped on our old camp of the 8"—very little wood and very cold. Thermometer went down to -42 below zero and froze. had to melt snow to make coffee. this is the coldest we have had yet. in fact I do not know how cold it was as we could not tell the mercury having froze. One man in the Co. had his feet frozen while on guard during the night and I can see lots of men riding in the ambulances with frozen hands and feet.**
>
> **Dec. 25 '76 Marched to the west of Pumkin Butt[e]s. very cold all day and horses giving out all along the road no more grain for them and no grass to amount to anything as the snow prevents the horses from grazing.**
>
> **Dec. 26. Broke camp at 10 AM and marched to the Cheyenne river Though we suffer much, every one is bearing it as well as possible for we know we have now good prospects of a good place for the winter.[12]**

Sgt. James Byron Kincaid also reported in his diary that the 1876 winter campaign was one of the worst. Kincaid's fortunes hit rock bottom as did the thermometer.

> **Christmas morning of 1876 was a morning that will be remembered by the men of the campaign as long as life exists. About two o'clock a.m. I awoke, being too cold to sleep longer; or as the boys term it—I froze out, and left the tent. The moon was shining and I saw the sentry was pacing back and forth in front of Gen. Crook's Quarters. I went over to him and asked if he had any fire, he said he would say not for there was not wood enough in 20 miles to boil a cup of coffee.**
>
> **"Did you freeze out?" he asked, "Well you might as well join the rest." "Who do you mean," I asked. "Why look down the valley; they are walking to keep from freezing to death." I did and in the pale moonlight I could see five or six hundred men walking to keep life in the bodies.**

"What is the meaning of this?" I asked; he told me I would soon find out if I stood there long. I asked him how cold it was. He thought we could go see for there was a thermometer outside the General's tent. But we were disappointed for looking at the instrument by the light of a match that the mercury had gone down to 42 degrees below zero and had broken the glass. I told him I thought it pretty tough and that I wished that I could find some wood.

"Well there is no wood! so you might as well go back to bed." Nothing doing I told him. Being too cold to sleep, was the reason that I had left it. He told me to join the gang which I did, walking and slapping my hands until morning, then we gathered sage brush enough to boil some coffee, and then the command moved on.

We had been on the march about three hours when the assistant wagon master rode up to the head of the command, and notified the Gen. that there was a teamster frozen to death.

"I expect he was drunk," said the General. "Well you go see an Orderly, and tell him to see about it, and tell the Commanding Officer of each company to report to me at once." Then turning to the Captain of the First Company, told him to detail two non-commissioned officers to ride along the column, and if they saw any of the men getting drowsy, to compel them to get off and walk.

About 3 p.m. we rounded the famous Butts point and when we descended the western side of the mountain it began to get warmer, and about dark we went in camp on Butts creek. Here there was plenty of cotton wood, and the men put up their tents and stoves, and built fires in them. Then the trouble began; for some of the men had frozen their feet and hands, and when they got to the fire and began to thaw out, it was a pitiful sight and not very comforting to hear them curse the army and every thing and every one that belonged to it.

The next morning when we broke camp there was a good many lead horses, as a big force of men were in the hospital wagons. That day we made 21 miles and after four days of hard travel we arrived at Ft. Fetterman. Here we got supplies, and some of the men began to forget the hardships they had just been through by taking a good breakfast. But some will never forget, and the next summer our trail could be followed by the dead horses and mules strung along the way.[13]

Even for John G. Bourke, an officer, the campaign proved memorable for its misery.

> **One of the most disagreeable days in my experience was Christmas, 1876. We were pushing across the Pumpkin Buttes, doing our best to get into bivouac and escape the fury of the elements, which seemed eager to devour us. Beards, moustaches, eye-lashes and eye-brows were frozen masses of ice. The keen air was filled with minute crystals, each cutting the tender skin like a razor, while feet and hands ached as if beaten with clubs. Horses and mules shivered while they stood in column, their flanks white with crystals of perspiration congealed on their bodies, and their nostrils bristling with icicles.[14]**

The officers did make an attempt at celebrating the day with some whiskey punch, Bourke noted in his diary.

> **December 25th. Xmas, Merry Xmas, made to bow under the chaperonage of old Father Winter. The cold was so bitter this morning that the mercury could not be coaxed out of the bulb but sullenly lay there coagulated. Considerable suffering from cold and numerous instances of frost-bite, but excepting one poor fellow who will have to lose his toes, none of any significance.**
>
> **Last night, General Crook invited General Mackenzie, Colonel Dodge, Colonel Townsend and the officers of his own staff to assist him in disposing of a hot whiskey punch prepared by Captain Eagan and Furey. After that to bed.[15]**

Richard I. Dodge.

Lt. Col. Richard I. Dodge, Twenty-third Infantry, summed up the day.

> **Take it all in all it is a Xmas long to be remembered, and I don't care ever to have another like it.[16]**

The efforts of the soldiers did not produce their desired result as Crazy Horse remained a free man.

Twenty-fifth infantrymen trying to keep warm around a Sibley stove, winter of 1890–91. Courtesy National Archives.

Fourteen years later the U.S. Army again confronted the Sioux. Fortunes had changed. No longer did the army have to hunt for the Indians—they were confined to reservations, easily reached from nearby rail lines.

For many soldiers, the weeks leading up to the Christmas holidays in 1890 had been spent waiting for something to happen—either peace or war. The Sioux, many of whom were engaged in the sacred and misunderstood Ghost Dance, did little to ease the tension in the soldier camps. That had to be provided by the troops themselves. First Sgt. Ragnar Theodor Ling-Vannerus, Seventh Cavalry, wrote of his camp's holiday preparations.

> The camp [at Pine Ridge] now began to assume a festive appearance. Every tent was decorated with firs and twigs, and long garlands of evergreens were stretched between the tents. At each end of the picket lines, sheaves were put up, and thousands of blackbirds, sparrows, and bullfinches flew twittering between the horses or sat happily on their backs and even heads in true companionship. In the kitchens everybody was busy; turkeys and geese were roasted or grilled and filled with apples and other delicacies, whole pigs were hung on the broaches, pastries and cakes were baked, and so on. . . .Eventually came the feast eagerly longed-for, and mighty was the eating and drinking among high and low. The officers established a kind of saloon by combining some tents in a row, in the middle of which was a long table, groaning under its abundant spread of both substantial and delicious foods, flanked by bottles and decanters of all calibres and colours, from Piper Heidseck to Old Rock and Rye Highland Whiskey. . . .Along the walls there were low seats covered with a mixed collection of skin rugs, in whose soft, warm furs it was delightful to rest, while speeches, toasts, and songs made time unnoticeably go by. There were also Christmas gifts from near and far, but funniest were those which one gave to one another and which, owing to a thorough knowledge of person, were perfectly adapted to hit the nail on the head and

to give rise to the most hilarious "contre-temps" and pranks, without in the least disturbing the mutual harmony. The iron bands of discipline were moderately loosened, and all through the camp one heard choir after choir, innocent laughter, and merry talk that interrupted the usual deserted emptiness of the nights. To many—a last Christmas feast. . . .

The day of December 26 opened up overcast and severe, snowflakes were falling here and there, but everything was quiet and a kind of mist seemed to be suspended over the countryside. The ordinary forenoon duties were going on as usual, but both officers and men seemed out of spirits, and even the memories of the Christmas festivities had lost their charm during this slow, depressing wait for the orders to march.[17]

Notes

[1] George H. Shirk, "Campaigning with Sheridan: A Farrier's Diary," *The Chronicles of Oklahoma* 37 (Spring 1959):91.

[2] Herman Werner, *On the Western Frontier with the United States Cavalry Fifty Years Ago* (Privately printed, 1934), 92.

[3] Ibid., 94-95.

[4] Diary no. 1, 1872, John Gregory Bourke Diary, 1872-96, United States Military Academy Library, West Point (hereafter cited as "Bourke diary" with number and year). Microfilm copies of the diary are held by the Nebraska State Historical Society and the Denver Public Library, which were examined for this work.

[5] David L. Spotts, *Campaigning With Custer and the Nineteenth Kansas Volunteer Cavalry on the Washita Campaign, 1868-'69*, E. A. Brininstool, ed. (Los Angeles: Wetzel Publishing Company, 1928), 86-88.

[6] Thomas T. Smith, ed., *A Dose of Frontier Soldiering: The Memoirs of Corporal E. A. Bode, Frontier Regular Infantry, 1877-1882* (Lincoln: University of Nebraska Press, 1994), 172-73.

[7] John Bigelow, Jr., *On the Bloody Trail of Geronimo*, Arthur Woodward, ed. (Los Angeles: Westernlore Press, 1958), 100-101.

[8] Robert C. Carriker, ed., "Thompson McFadden's Diary of an Indian Campaign, 1874," *Southwestern Historical Quarterly* 75 (Oct. 1971):232.

[9] Gene M. Gressley, ed., "A Soldier with Crook: The Letters of Henry R. Porter," *Montana The Magazine of Western History* 8 (July 1958):43.

[10] Joe F. Taylor, ed., "The Indian Campaign on the Staked Plains, 1874-1875: Military Correspondence from War Department Adjutant General's Office, File 2815-1874," *Panhandle-Plains Historical Review* 34 (1961):147-48.

[11] Sherry L. Smith, *Sagebrush Soldier: Private William Earl Smith's View of the Sioux War of 1876* (Norman: University of Oklahoma Press, 1989), 121-22,123.

[12] Thomas R. Buecker, ed., "The Journals of James S. McClellan, 1st Sgt., Company H., 3rd Cavalry," *Annals of Wyoming* 57 (Spring 1985):32.

[13] "Final Chapter in the Diary of J. B. Kinkaid," *Winners of the West*, June 1940.

[14] John G. Bourke, *Mackenzie's Last Fight with the Cheyennes: A Winter Campaign in Wyoming and Montana* (Bellevue, Nebr.: The Old Army Press, 1970), 41-42.

[15] Bourke diary, no. 15, 1876.

[16] Dodge diary, courtesy the Richard Irving Dodge Papers, Everett D. Graff Collection, The Newberry Library, Chicago; quoted in Smith, *Sagebrush Soldier*, 123.

[17] Christer Lindberg, ed., "Foreigners in Action at Wounded Knee," *Nebraska History* 71 (Fall 1990):172-73.

Chapter Three

Christmastime Perils

"The depressing news was strong enough to cast a deep gloom over us."

When it comes to achieving a military objective, there is no stopping to celebrate the holidays. Some of the most perilous events took place during the Christmas season. The two presented here—the Fetterman Fight and the Wounded Knee Massacre—are powerful reminders of this fact.

Four days before Christmas 1866 the frontier army suffered a shocking defeat at the hands of Red Cloud's Sioux. The tribe bitterly resented the Bozeman Trail, which ran north through their best hunting grounds (now Wyoming) to the Montana gold fields, and the forts that guarded it. Residents of the Bozeman forts, especially at Fort Phil Kearny and those on the wagon trains hauling lumber for its construction, experienced an almost constant state of siege from the Sioux.

Unfortunately the fort's inhabitants also had to bear intense personality clashes among its officers. A young firebrand, Capt. William J. Fetterman, urged immediate action against the Indians, recklessly boasting that he could ride

"The Indian Battle and Massacre Near Fort Philip Kearney, Dacotah Territory, December 21, 1866." *Harper's Weekly* gave the nation a fanciful depiction of the Fetterman Fight in its March 23, 1867, issue.

through the entire Sioux nation with a company of men. Col. Henry B. Carrington, commander of the Eighteenth Infantry, believed that the over-whelming power of the Sioux and northern Cheyennes dictated more caution.

On December 21, 1866, Fetterman and Lt. George W. Grummond led seventy-nine men from behind the post's pallisaded walls to relieve the wood train. Red Cloud's warriors sprang a classic decoy maneuver, and when Fetterman disobeyed orders and pursued the Indians, his whole command quickly perished.

The situation at Fort Kearny was precarious and immediate reinforcements were essential, although the nearest relief was at Fort Laramie, some 236 miles away. John "Portugee" Phillips, a civilian employee of the quartermaster, felt terrible sorrow for Frances Grummond, the young, pregnant widow of Lieutenant Grummond, and volunteered to ride for help. He told her:

> **I am going to Laramie for help, with despatches, as special messenger, if it costs me my life. I am going for your sake! Here is my wolf robe. I brought it for you to keep and remember me by it if you never see me again.**[1]

The Christmas ride of Portugee Phillips became a western classic. Accompanied by others for portions of his journey, Phillips traveled the last leg alone and carried the messages through to Fort Laramie. Capt. David Gordon, Second Cavalry, recalled Phillips's arrival on Christmas night.

Portugee Phillips. Courtesy Wyoming Division of Cultural Resources, Cheyenne.

> **It was on Christmas Night, 11 P.M., when a full-dress garrison ball was progressing, and everybody appeared superlatively happy, enjoying the dance, notwithstanding the snow was from ten to fifteen inches deep on level, and the thermometer registered twenty-five degrees below zero, when a huge form, dressed in buffalo overcoat, pants, gauntlets and cap, accompanied by an orderly, desired to see the commanding officer. The dress of the man, and at this hour looking for the commanding officer, made a deep impression upon the officers and others that happened to get a glimpse of him, in this strange garb, dropping into our full-dress garrison ball at this unseasonable hour.**[2]

The bodies of Fetterman and his mutilated men had to be recovered, and Colonel Carrington set out to reclaim them. Fears of renewed Indian attacks led him to issue a somber instruction to the soldiers left behind.

Capt. William J. Fetterman. Courtesy American Heritage Center, University of Wyoming.

Col. Henry B. Carrington. Courtesy Wyoming Division of Cultural Resources, Cheyenne.

Lt. George W. Grummond. Courtesy Wyoming Division of Cultural Resources, Cheyenne.

> **If, in my absence, Indians in overwhelming numbers attack, put the women and children in the magazine with supplies of water, bread, crackers and other supplies that seem best, and, in the event of a last desperate struggle, destroy all together, rather than have any captured alive.**[3]

Following the recovery of the bodies, Frances Grummond wrote of the ensuing days at the fort, understandably with no mention of the holidays.

> **And then the horrors of the following days, the making of coffins and digging in the hard, frozen earth for a burial place, when the cold was so intense that the men worked in fifteen-minute reliefs, and a guard was constantly on the alert lest Indians should interrupt their service.**
>
> **One-half of the headquarters building, which was my temporary home, was unfinished, and this part was utilized by carpenters for making pine cases for the dead. I knew that my husband's coffin was being made, and the sound of hammers and the grating of saws was torture to my sensitive nerves.**[4]

Frances Grummond (Carrington). Courtesy American Heritage Center, University of Wyoming.

In the days following the tragedy, Colonel Carrington's wife, Margaret, took in the young widow Grummond and later wrote poignantly of that tense and terrible Christmas.

The holidays were sad as they were cold. Lights were burned in all quarters, and one non-commissioned officer was always on duty in each building, so that in case of alarm, there could not be an instant's delay in the use of the whole command. Each company knew its place and the distribution of the loop-holes; the gunners slept in tents near their guns, and all things were ripe for the destruction of assailants should any venture to attack.

The constant and drifting snow-storms soon so lifted by their crests by the west flank of the stockade that officers walked over its trunks, and when a trench ten feet wide was cleared, the next snow or wind would fill it, as only snow can snow and winds can blow in that suburb of Cloud Peak, the home of perpetual snow.

The men themselves, who, at the October muster, looked forward to the holidays and December muster with glad anticipations, forbore all demonstrations usual to such a period, and sensibly felt the weight of the great loss incurred.

Of the sergeants who had distinguished themselves in the previous war, or had actively operated in the labors of 1866, nearly all of the most prominent had fallen: Lange, a martinet, trim, upright, and soldierly; Bissell, calm, mature, and carrying into his profession the sturdy habits of business which had marked his life in Chicago before a hasty indiscretion impelled him to the army; Smith, the pride of the mounted infantry; Morgan, and many others, deserve an enduring monument over their last resting-place no less than heroes of more exalted stations from more memorable battlefields.

The whole garrison shared the gloom. Charades, tableaus, Shakspearian [sic] readings, the usual muster evening levee at the Colonel's, and all the social reunions which had been anticipated as bringing something pleasant, and in the similitude of civilized life, were dropped as unseasonable and almost unholy. Present and exacting duty admitted no dalliance with pleasures that were at other times rational and refreshing; and a calm, sedate, but genial sympathy brought most to a closer fraternity, almost confirming the sacred proverb, "That it is better to go to the house of mourning than to the house of feasting."[5]

Following the death of Margaret Carrington in 1870, Frances Grummond corresponded with Colonel Carrington, and the two married in 1871.

Rumors of the Fetterman defeat made their way to Fort Bridger, present-day Wyoming. Elizabeth Burt, wife of Capt. Andrew S. Burt, recalled the shadow that fell over Christmas 1866 at Fort Bridger and her efforts to make a festive holiday for their son, Andrew Gano.

Through newspapers and the stage line, accounts came of increasing trouble at Fort Phil Kearny. The Sioux Indians had determined to unite in their efforts to drive the soldiers from their fine hunting grounds and to prevent a road being opened through the land that had always been exclusively their own. The depressing news was strong enough to cast a deep gloom over us; but as Christmas approached, for our boy's sake, we made as great an effort as possible to enter into the spirit of the season.

We made different kinds of candy, as we could buy as much sugar as was needful from the Commissary. Judge Carter had brought a small supply of gifts in his ox train. His present to Andrew Gano was the first mechanical toy we had ever seen. It was a boy who walked amazingly well and surprised even us older people.

The stockings were hung in the wide, open fireplace, down which Santa Claus could descend with ease. Plenty of snow made splendid traveling for his eight tiny reindeer. My six Sunday School scholars were made happy by homemade candy, ice cream, cookies and doughnuts.

A delicious Christmas dinner at Judge Carter's hospitable board helped greatly to make the day a happy one for us, so far away from friends.

The holiday time thus happily begun was of short duration for only a few days after Christmas we began to hear mysterious rumors of a fight which had taken place near Fort Phil Kearny in which the Indians had defeated our troops. We refused to believe them at first, but they continued. It was the Indian "underground" which carried the news from valley to valley, across mountain ranges, and delivered it in vague whisperings at the sutler's store through the "friendlies" who came in to trade. We hardly mentioned the subject except to say, "It can't be true. Surely it can't be true." Each tried to be hopeful before his neighbor but none succeeded in concealing his anxiety.

In our fear we little realized the actual truth, so when the official report arrived we were only partially prepared for the

heartbreaking news—"Colonel Fetterman, Captain Brown, 18th Infantry, Lieutenant Grummond, 2nd Cavalry, and 78 men massacred near Phil Kearny"—this was a shock that reached the very soul of comradeship and from which it seemed we could not recover. These were among the friends from whom we had parted at the Platte River the previous June when they separated from us to go with Colonel Carrington to build Fort Phil Kearny in what is now Wyoming. Little did we imagine the horrible fate awaiting them when we said goodbye that peaceful June evening.[6]

The 1890 Ghost Dance troubles at Pine Ridge Reservation and the tragedy of Wounded Knee still weigh heavily on the Sioux people. That these events occurred during the Christmas season offers additional poignancy. The Christmas ride of Guy Henry and "Henry's Brunettes" may stir some poetic notions, but it merely sets the stage for the descriptions of the little Episcopal chapel, still gaily decorated with Christmas greenery, that became the hospital for some of the Indian survivors of December 29.

Col. Guy V. Henry's Ninth Cavalry, one of the famed "buffalo soldier" regiments, faced a cold Christmas Eve march in the midst of the escalating troubles. An anonymous member of the column, under the name "Sioux," wrote:

> At 2 P.M., Wednesday, Dec. 24, Col. Henry's battalion of the 9th Cavalry moved out at the trot to the point to intercept a band of Indians who had escaped from Sumner's command. They made a night march, with their pack train, and covered 50 miles—a pleasant way to spend Christmas eve, and the thoughts of many a weary one on the cold night's march fled to the ones at home keeping their Christmas in another way. They are now encamped in the Bad Lands at Harney Springs, covering the supposed route of the hostiles, but as Indians do not corral very well, nor run into traps set for them, it is not thought they will run into any such. . . .[7]

Even the Indians seemed a little taken aback by the troops' movements during the bitter holiday weather, as one anonymous correspondent reported.

> To-day it has blown a gale, but under our cover we have been protected. With glasses we could see the hostiles yesterday taking down their tepees to move in. It would be a good idea to have troops go up into this impregnable position and

get the lay of the land. The scouts say the Indians were much surprised to see on Christmas Day troops within six miles of them. . . .[8]

Years later Pvt. Grant C. Topping, Troop F, Sixth Cavalry, recalled the continuing search for Big Foot's band of Sioux.

One of Guy V. Henry's Ninth cavalrymen. NSHS-W938-119-43A.

Your letter received this morning and as you asked me to do a favor by writing to you in regard to Battle of Wounded Knee will try to illustrate as near as possible what took place and the hardships the boys of the 6th went through.

On December 24 a message was received that Big Foot was moving south on the Deep Fork trail. At this time we were on White Horse Creek. A courier from the 7th U.S. cavalry . . .now came into camp being nearly overcome by fatigue and hard riding. Boots and saddles were sounded and Colonel Carr ordered a forced crossing over the river near Cheyenne which was covered by floating ice. No obstacles were too great as we were after the redskins. Those who participated in this charge will never forget it as even the alkaline pools were frozen, the weather being so cold. Christmas morning found us on the pinnacle of one of the highest points in the badlands from which we would see the country for miles around.[9]

Guy V. Henry (seated, fifth from right) **and the officers of the Ninth Cavalry during the Pine Ridge Campaign, 1890–91.** NSHS-W938:21-1.

Col. Guy V. Henry wrote of the Ninth Cavalry's Christmas Eve spent on the trail of Big Foot.

The afternoon of December 24 an order reached us to move out at once to head off Big Foot—an Indian chief—and his band, who had escaped from our troops, and, it was supposed, would join the hostiles in the Bad Lands; and this we were to prevent. So at 2 P.M. the "general" sounded—a signal which meant to strike our tents and pack our mules and wagons. The latter were to follow us, escorted by one troop. Soon "boots and saddles" rang out, when horses were saddled, line formed, and then, with three troops and with two Hotchkiss guns of the First Artillery, under Lieutenant Hayden, we commenced our march of fifty miles, expecting to reach our goal before daylight. Only a half-hundred miles! It does not seem far on paper, but on the back of a trotting horse on a cold winter's night it is not to be laughed at. On we dashed through the agency, buoyed by the hearty cheers and "A merry Christmas!" given us by the comrades we were leaving behind to revel by the camp-fires, while we rode on by moonlight to meet the foe. Every heart went out in sympathy with us, every one waved his hat and cheered as we rode out on the plains—perhaps to glory, perchance to death. Proud and gallant the troopers looked, more as if going on parade than like men riding forth, it might be, to meet a soldiers death. It made one's heart beat quicker. . . .

Little did we think at that time that within less than one week some of the gallant men we were leaving behind would be killed by the very band we sought, while we should be

saved. After riding for two hours, alternately at a trot and a walk, a short halt was made for the men to make coffee and to give the horses a feed. Then the march was continued, and on and on we sped, that cold, moonlight Christmas eve. The words, "Peace on earth, good will toward men," rang in our ears as we pushed on with hostile intent toward the red man. The night was beautiful with the clear moon, but so cold that water froze solid in our canteens, not withstanding the constant shaking. Crossing a narrow bridge, a pack-mule was shoved off by its crowded comrades, and falling on the ice of Wounded Knee Creek, broke a hole, smashed a box of hardtack, but gathered himself together, and ambled off, smiling serenely at having received no damage to his body.

Here we passed abandoned ranches, the owners driven off by threats or fear of the Indians; here we were at the scene of the ghost-dances, where the Indians were taught that the Messiah would appear, rid the country of the white man, and bring plenty to the Indian; that the common cotton ghost shirt worn was bullet-proof; while in every other possible way the medicine men worked upon the fanaticism of the deluded creature. We saw at a distance stray cattle, whose spectral appearance almost led us to believe in ghosts, if not in ghost shirts, and an examination was made to see whether or not they were Indians waiting on their ponies to attack us.

To cross White River we had to take a plunge from solid ice to mid-channel water, and then rode to Cottonwood Springs, at the base of the position of the Indians in the Bad Lands. We reached this place at 4 A.M., and threw ourselves on the ground for rest, knowing that to obtain wood and water for breakfast Christmas morning we should have to march eight miles. And this is the way the Ninth Cavalry squadron spent Christmas eve of 1890.[10]

At Pine Ridge Agency, South Dakota, Christmas celebrations with the Sioux Indian children were ongoing. Thisba Hutson Morgan, a teacher at the United States government boarding school at Pine Ridge Agency, wrote of the irony of the situation.

On this same Christmas Eve, there had been set up in the little Protestant Episcopal Church at the Agency, the Church of the Holy Cross, a huge cedar tree reaching to the ceiling. It was lighted by candles and a large star at the top. It was festooned with yards and yards of strung popcorn and ladies with little bags of fruit, candy, and nuts. Colorful scarfs and

handkerchiefs for the boys floated from the branches, and beautiful French dolls for the girls peeped like fairies from everywhere. The two hundred pupils attending the Ogalalla Boarding School were having their Christmas celebration that the beautiful story of the Christ Child might be impressed upon them and the joy of Christmas be theirs. The lovely French dolls, one hundred of them, had come from the missionary-minded women of Christ Church in New Orleans. It was heartwarming to see the faces of the Indian children brighten and their eyes sparkle as they examined and caressed their gifts, never forgetting the quiet decorum so carefully instilled into them by their grandmothers that was so often mistaken by the white people for indifference or vacuity.

This was the first of a series of such services. Each day during the Christmas octave, the tree was to be redecorated and each night the Indians from the outlying districts, where the Church had sub-missions, were coming in their turn to the Mother Church for Christmas gifts. The warm heavy practical gifts of clothing for the oldsters and vestments for the Indian Catechists in charge of the sub-missions came in the most part from New York and New England. . . .

Five times the tree had been laden with gifts. Four times the beautiful Christmas service had been given in the Sioux language; then on December 29th, like a thunderbolt, came news of the terrible battle of Wounded Knee, stunning the peaceful Indians and the whites alike.[11]

Elaine Goodale, also at Pine Ridge Agency, later to become the wife of the famous Santee Sioux physician Charles Eastman, who attended to the victims, left an account of the terrible aftermath of the massacre.

I look back now upon that Christmas season of 1890-91 as upon a dream. Even at the time, it seemed unreal. The pageant of war all about us—the neat rows of Sibley tents, the trenches and breastworks, the buffalo-coated sentinel who faced us at every turn—all this where there had been no "outbreak" at all, and none as we believed was threatened, has a very singular effect. The Indians gathered every day in little groups to watch the troops parade, as if it had been a show provided for their amusement!

We tried to go on with our occupations as usual. The accustomed preparations were made for the Christmas festival. Cedar was woven into garlands, the Christmas anthems were

practiced nightly, great boxes of toys and clothing were opened and sorted for distribution—all with assumed cheerfulness, but not without a secret sense of dread and anxiety.

A Christmas tree of generous size had been set up in the Episcopal chapel at the agency, and it was arranged to dress it on several successive nights, for the numerous congregations represented in the "friendly" encampment. In the meantime, a detachment of troops had been sent out to meet and disarm Big Foot's approaching band; but we on the frontier knew nothing of the plans of the commanding officer—knew almost less than the readers of the New York papers about what was happening in our midst.

We were labeling gifts and filling candybags for the children when the first flying rumors reached us of the carnage at Wounded Knee. These early reports were even worse than the reality, for we understood that the cavalry had been cut off from reaching the agency—Wounded Knee creek is eighteen miles distant—and that we were at the mercy of a maddened horde of Indians. . . .

At ten o'clock in the evening the Seventh cavalry came in with their own wounded, and some thirty wounded Indian prisoners, more than half of them women and children, moaning with anguish, chilled, half-starved and wholly broken-hearted—for out of each family, as a rule, there were but one or two survivors.

We gathered the poor creatures into the chapel, with its ropes of fragrant cedar and its loaded Christmas tree, and there they were warmed and fed, their ghastly wounds were dressed, and there for many days we cared for the suffering and the dying—for many of the injuries were mortal. . . .

It was a strange sight, and one that can never be forgotten—these poor fanatics lying helpless and wounded, at the blessed Christmas-tide, in a Christian house of worship, gazing with wondering and, after a while, with comprehending eyes at the glowing cross in the chancel window, while they began to realize perhaps, at last, that the white man's Messiah and the Indian's Messiah are one, and that He has come to the poor Indian in his hour of need.[12]

Episcopal Bishop W. H. Hare, who visited the church in the days following the fight, commented on the scene of horror.

[O]n entering the church, two sights presented themselves. On the church floor, instead of the pews on either side of the

"We gathered the poor creatures into the chapel, with its ropes of fragrant cedar. . . ." **Treating the Indians from Wounded Knee.** Courtesy South Dakota State Historical Society.

aisle, two rows of bleeding, groaning, wounded men, women and children; tending them two military surgeons and a native physician assisted by the missionary and his helpers, assiduity and tenderness marking all. Above, the Christmas green was still hanging. To one of my moods they seemed a mockery to all my faith and hope; to another they seemed an inspiration still singing, though in a minor key, "Peace, good will to men."[13]

Notes

[1] Frances C. Carrington, *My Army Life: A Soldier's Wife at Fort Phil Kearny* (Boulder, Colo.: Pruett Publishing Company, 1990), 149. Originally published as *My Army Life and the Fort Phil Kearney Massacre.*

[2] Robert R. Larson, "Christmas and New Year's Holidays on the Wyoming Frontier," manuscript in the research files of Fort Laramie National Historic Site, Fort Laramie, Wyoming.

[3] Carrington, *My Army Life,* 153-54.

[4] Ibid., 155.

[5] Margaret Irvin Carrington, *Ab-sa-ra-ka, Home Of The Crows: Being the Experience of an Officer's Wife on the Plains* (Philadelphia: J. B. Lippincott & Co., 1869), 213-15.

[6] Merrill J. Mattes, *Indians, Infants and Infantry: Andrew and Elizabeth Burt on the Frontier* (Denver: The Old West Publishing Company, 1960), 83-84.

[7] *Army and Navy Journal* (hereafter cited as *ANJ*), Jan. 3, 1891.

[8] Ibid.

[9] *Winners of the West,* Feb. 1925.

[10] *Harper's Weekly,* Dec. 26, 1896.

[11] Thisba Hutson Morgan, "Reminiscences of My Days in the Land of the Ogallala Sioux," *South Dakota Department of History Report and Historical Collections* 29 (1958):52.

[12] Elaine Goodale Eastman, "Christmas Among the Ghost-Dancers," *The Midland Monthly* 2 (Dec. 1894):437-38.

[13] M. A. DeWolfe Howe, *The Life and Labors of Bishop Hare* (New York: Sturgis & Walton Company, 1913), 240; the original account appeared in "Bishop's Record," *The Church News,* Jan. 1891.

Chapter Four

FOOD

"He was thrown into a state of dismay on learning plum pudding had been added to the list."

As with many holidays, we often associate a happy Christmas with traditionally prepared foods. The typical soldier's diet consisted of beans, hardtack, salt bacon, and coffee. Traditional Christmas fare was not always easy to come by on the frontier, especially fresh fruits and vegetables. Army rations did not include milk, butter, and eggs. Soldiers could use their own money to buy these items, when available, from sutlers and post traders. Many posts undertook the planting of their own vegetable gardens.

For the holidays, however, extraordinary efforts were made to produce a home cooked meal of favorite foods. Individual military companies planned and prepared for a feast months in advance. What a difference the presence of a nearby railroad made to a Christmas feast. Traditional customs, excessively Victorian to begin with, may have been amplified in the American West. Forts far from a rail line substituted ingenuity for iced oysters and champagne. Fish and wild game provided a feast that we would consider exotic when everyone craved good old Tom Turkey.

In order to ensure there would be a feast at Fort Laramie in 1879, the post adjutant requested all officers promptly place their orders for holiday trimmings.

1900 Christmas dinner of Company C, Third Infantry, Fort Snelling.
Courtesy Minnesota Historical Society.

> There will be a light wagon leaving this Post in a few days for Cheyenne W.T. All Commissioned Officers and others requiring Turkeys Chickens Cranberries or any other articles for Christmas, will please notify the Post Adjutant at once, the number (in pounds) of each article they require.[1]

Katherine Gibson, wife of Capt. Francis M. Gibson, Seventh Cavalry, wrote in her memoirs of the extra efforts the mailman made to deliver fresh, unbroken eggs for her Christmas meal at Fort Abraham Lincoln, Dakota Territory.

> The refreshments would be sandwiches, cake, and candy, lemonade made from the usual citric acid crystals, and, of course, ice cream evolved from condensed milk, whipped-up gelatine, and the whites of eggs. The eggs by the way, wrapped in cotton, were brought from Bismarck by the mailman, who, to keep such precious articles from freezing, always carried them inside his buckskin shirt, against his bare breast.[2]

John Bigelow. Courtesy U.S. Military Academy, West Point.

Lt. John Bigelow, Tenth Cavalry, stationed at Fort Davis, Texas, recalled an 1884 Christmas dinner, the menu made possible by the post's relative proximity to the Gulf of Mexico.

> We took dinner with the Ayers. It was the most refined and enjoyable entertainment I have been to since my return here. It was quite like civilization. We had raw oysters (from Galveston, I presume) soup, turkey and vegetables, plum pudding & a cold blanc mange-like dish and fruit & nuts, with Claret & Cook's Imperial. The cooking and serving were both good.[3]

Two years later, Lieutenant Bigelow found himself stationed at Mowry Mine, Arizona. Preparations for a Christmas dinner in the field were a little more crude.

> The next thing that claimed my attention was the roast pig for dinner. There being no one in camp who knew how to make a barbecue, I had got the packer, who had had some experience, he said, in cooking beef's heads, to undertake the cooking of my piece of pork. He had a hole dug in the ground about eighteen inches deep, and a layer of bright embers put in the bottom.

On this he put a layer of gunny sacks, and on this the meat. He then covered the meat with gunny sacks and the sacks with embers and ashes and earth. This was accomplished about "taps" last night. At 1:15 to-day, when the cut was taken out by mean of cords passed under it—the operation suggesting the reversal of a burial—it was done to a turn, and exhaled a delicious aroma. A piece presented to me for dinner proved the most savory pork viand that I have ever tasted.[4]

Dr. John V. Lauderdale, post surgeon at Fort Bridger, noted in a letter to his sister in 1865 the postponement of the Christmas dinner.

The poultry and things which were to form the more substantial part of the christmas dinner not arriving by the coach till late in the day, the dinner was put off till the next day at four in the P.M. when we sat down to a good old fashioned collation. And in the evening we had a very pleasant time in the parlor. No cards but singing and story telling.[5]

The following episode took place nearer Santa's North Pole than any other presented in this volume. Lt. Adolphus W. Greely, Fifth Cavalry, commanded the Lady Franklin Bay Expedition or Greely Expedition, 1881-1884, which established the farthest north U.S. weather station. Fort Conger, the expedition's base camp, sat above the Arctic Circle, well beyond the usual range of the frontier army. Nevertheless, the popularity of the expedition led to a few special gifts at Christmastime 1881.

The preparation of the Christmas dinner was commenced several days in advance, as from its extensive character much extra labor was entailed upon Frederick, who was the extra cook.

Unfortunately he burned his arm quite badly on the 23d, but, dispite [sic] his condition, requested that he be permitted to complete his tour of duty. Long, who was considered the especial cook of the party, with his customary cheerfulness, assisted Frederick in the preparation of this important meal.

The capacity of our excellent cooking range, with its large ovens and hot water boilers, was thoroughly tested on Christmas day. When Frederick, the cook, had planned out a place for cooking the many dishes for the great dinner, he was thrown into a state of dismay on learning that plum pudding had been added to the list. He came to me, saying that he did not see how he [could] cook this dish, as his range was taxed to its utmost; and he was much relieved to learn that Mrs.

Greely had sent a case of pudding as a Christmas present for the expedition.

The menu for the dinner was as follows: Mock-turtle soup, salmon, fricasseed guillemot, spiced musk-ox tongue, crab-salad, roast beef, eider-ducks, tenderloin of musk-ox, potatoes, asparagus, green corn, green peas, cocoanut-pie, jelly-take [cake], plum-pudding with wine-sauce, several kinds of ice-cream, grapes, cherries, pine-apples, dates, figs, nuts, candies, coffee, chocolate. Eggnog was served to the party in moderate quantities, and an extra allowance of rum was also issued in celebration of the day.

The candies, plum-pudding, and cigars were the most appreciated, not only for the satisfaction they afforded the taste, but as being gifts from thoughtful friends. The cigars came from an army lady who knew the weakness of the rank and file for the consoling weed, and the candies were from a leading confectioner of New York City.[6]

This joyous meal was to be one of the few happy times for the Greely Expedition. Of the initial twenty-four members, only six survived.

A sampler of menus from various forts showed the universal desire to present a truly memorable Christmas meal.

Fort Leavenworth, Kansas, 1877:

Enclosed please find our bill of fare of our Christmas dinner. As you made a mistake in giving credit to Co. H, instead of Co. A, on our Thanksgiving dinner, we want no mistake this time. We would also like mentioned that Col. Coppinger's Company A, 23d Inf., live better and feel better than any company in the regiment.

Bill of Fare.—Soup: Oyster. Meats: Roasted turkey stuffed and gravy, roast beef and gravy, cold boiled ham. Vegetables: Mashed potatoes, mashed turnips, stewed tomatoes, stewed onions. Relishes: Spiced tomatoes, cold slaw, cranberry sauce. Pastry: Mince pie, apple pie, cranberry tarts, current [sic] cake, raisin cake, marble cake, gold cake, silver cake, lemon drops, doughnuts, gingerbread. Tea.[7]

Plum Pudding, No. 1

The ingredients of this pudding, with the exception of the eggs and milk, should be prepared the day before the pudding is to be made.

    2 qts. sifted flour

    2 qts. bread crumbs

    four pounds suet, freed from fiber and chopped moderately fine

    four pounds raisins, picked, seeded, chopped, and dredged with flour

    sixteen eggs, whites and yolks beaten separately

    two qts. sweet milk (or equivalent of condensed milk)

    1/4 lb. citron, cut fine and dredged with flour

    grated rind of one lemon

    two nutmegs, grated

    1 Tbsp. ground ginger

    1 Tbsp. ground cinnamon

    1 tsp. ground cloves

Into a deep pan or dish put the ingredients in the following order, incorporating them thoroughly: First, the beaten yolks of the eggs; then one-half the milk; then the flour, bread crumbs, suet, spices, and lemon rind; then the remainder of the milk, or as much of it as will make a thick batter; then the beaten whites or the eggs; and last the dredged fruit.

Beat the mixture for thirty minutes, put it into the prepared bag or bags, and boil seven hours. Serve hot with sauce.

The above recipe is enough for thirty men.

Recipe from *Manual for Army Cooks* (1896).

Alice Kirk Grierson's cookbook was saved and is preserved by the Fort Davis National Historic Site. Her original recipe for gingerbread appears in the first paragraph.

Gingerbread

1-1/2 cups molasses, into which, stir until it foams, 3 even teaspoons of soda, 1 cup sugar, 1 scant cup of butter, 2 large eggs, not beaten separately, 1-1/2 cups sour milk, ginger to taste, 3-1/2 cups flour. Bake either in small cakes or in sheets. Part lard can be used if butter is scant.

Cream butter and sugar together. Beat in eggs. Stir baking soda into molasses and mix until foamy. Add molasses mixture to creamed mixture. Sift flour and ginger together, and add to creamed mixture, alternately with the sour milk. Pour batter into two greased cake pans and bake in a 375 degree oven for 35 minutes or until done.

From *An Army Wife's Cookbook*, compiled and edited by Mary L. Williams.

A wide array of food was served at the 1904 Christmas dinner of the Seventh Battery at Fort Riley. Courtesy Joseph J. Pennell Collection, Kansas Collection, University of Kansas Libraries.

Fort Coeur d'Alene, Idaho, 1881:

> **Company A is to have seven kinds of meat for dinner on Christmas. They lately added the last of the seven by dressing a fine specimen of the porcine species weighing 330 pounds.**[8]

Buffalo soldiers celebrated at Fort Davis, Texas, in 1883.

> **A number of pleasant diversions have occurred with the post during the holiday week, the most noticeable of which were the dinner and ball given by Troop B, Tenth Cavalry, on Christmas. The menu for dinner was:**
>
> **Tomato soup, soda and oyster crackers, egg-nog. Meats—Roasted pigs, baked pork, roast venison and antelope; roasted turkey and chicken stuffed with giblets, with celery dressing; boiled ham, ham sandwiches. Vegetables—Baked potato, corn, tomatoes, maccaroni. Salads—Potato salad, chicken salad, celery salad. Relishes—Celery, water cress, pickles, mustard, canned apples, currant jelly, cranberry sauce, marmalade. Desserts—Apples, pears, peaches, oranges, bannanas, pine apple, pumplin, and apple pies; wine and lemon jellies, cocoanut, jelly, pound and fruit cakes; coffee, tea and cigars.**
>
> **Among many other things constituting the courses and of which we have not the space to notice were an abundance of nice butter and city baked bread. We cannot, however, but**

notice the beautifully decorated dining room, the elegant tableware, viz: seventy-two silver plated quart bowls, plated knives, forks, and spoons, six-bottle castors, six pickle stands, six syrup pitchers, six mustard pots, all of the best quaudruple plate. The tables, five in number, were each sixteen feet long, covered by exquisite red and white table cloths. Two beautiful Christmas trees laden with every variety of fruits, &c., added very materially to the decorations of the room. The dining room was visited by the officers and ladies of the post with their friends, all of whom joined in complimenting the energy of troop B in preparing such a bountiful and luxurious repast, after which the troop, with its many invited guests, did ample justice to the occasion.[9]

Fort Ringgold, Texas, 1886:

Christmas Day was warm and bright. The companies of the post all sat down to a bountiful spread of good things. The bill of fare of Troop I, Eighth Cavalry, comprised the following:

Meats—Turkey, with cranberry sauce; venison, with mayonaise sauce; chicken, roast pork.

Vegetables—Cabbage, mashed potatoes, French peas, mashed turnips, green corn, tomatoes.

Pastry—Apple pie, cranberry pie, mince pie, lemon pie.

Dessert—Marble cake, jelly cake, gold cake, silver cake, oranges and soft-shell almonds.

The tables were inspected by the officers of the post as the men were seated at dinner. Our commanding officer, Major Parke, was much pleased with the display, and highly complimented Sergeant Brannan, who is in charge of the mess, on the arrangement of the tables.

The cakes were presented to the troop by Mrs. William F. Hempel, our first sergeant's wife, and were pronounced excellent by all.

In addition to the other good things, each man was provided with a quart bottle of beer, which was presented by our troop saddler, James Patterson, who, by the way, will in a few days complete twenty-five years of continued service. He has been in the troop since the regiment was organized.[10]

Fort Leavenworth, Kansas, 1891:

A member of the provost guard, Fort Leavenworth, sends us the following appetizing menu for the guard on Christmas. It ought to stimulate the recruiting business:

Breakfast

Pork chops, French fried potatoes, cake, cookies, bread and butter, coffee and chocolate.

Dinner

Roast turkey with dressing, roast goose with cranberry sauce, fresh fish, escallopped oysters, mashed potatoes, baked sweet potatoes, green peas, succotash, stewed tomatoes, lettuce, pickled cucumbers, beets, beans and chow-chow, catsup and Worcestershire sauce. Dessert: Sponge cake, blanc mange, currant jelly, mince pie, apples, lemonade, tea and coffee.

Supper

Cold sliced fresh pork, cheese, apples, mince and custard pie, bread and butter, tea. Miscellaneous: Cigars, cider, almonds, picans [sic], filberts, English walnuts and candy.

Our correspondent informs us that the latch string of the provost guard is always out, and that any man may join in the confident expectation of always leaving the table well-satisfied.[11]

Cooks took great pains to prepare special foods, but as most could attest, cooking "disasters" unfortunately happened during the holidays. Frances M. A. Roe, wife of Lt. Fayette W. Roe, Third Infantry, noted her problems with some overanxious eaters at Fort Lyon, Colorado, in 1871.

They have such a charming custom in the Army of going along the line Christmas morning and giving each other pleasant greetings and looking at the pretty things everyone has received. This is a rare treat out here, where we are so far from shops and beautiful Christmas displays. We all went to the bachelors' quarters, almost everyone taking over some little remembrance—homemade candy, cakes, or something of that sort.

I had a splendid cake to send over that morning, and I will tell you just what happened to it. At home we always had a large fruit cake made for the holidays, long in advance, and I thought I would have one this year as near like it as possible. But it seemed that the only way to get it was to make it. So, about four weeks ago, I commenced. It was quite an undertak-

ing for me, as I had never done anything of the kind, and perhaps I did not go about it the easiest way, but I knew how it should look when done, and of course I knew precisely how it should taste. Eliza makes delicious every-day cake, but was no assistance whatever with the fruit cake, beyond encouraging me with the assurance that would not matter in the least if it should be heavy.

Well, for two long, tiresome days I worked over that cake, preparing with my own fingers every bit of the fruit, which I consider was a fine test of perseverance and staying qualities. After the ingredients were all mixed together there seemed to be enough for a whole regiment, so we decided to make two cakes of it. They looked lovely when baked, and just right, and smelled so good, too! I wrapped them in nice white paper that had been wet with brandy, and put them carefully away—one in a stone jar, the other in a tin box—and felt that I had done a remarkably fine bit of housekeeping. The bachelors have been exceedingly kind to me, and I rejoiced at having a nice cake to send them Christmas morning. But alas! I forgot that the little house was fragrant with the odor of spice and fruit, and that there was a man about who was ever on the lookout for good things to eat. It is a shame that those cadets at West Point are so starved. They seem to be simply famished for months after they graduate.

It so happened that there was choir practice that very evening, and that I was at the chapel an hour or so. When I returned, I found the three bachelors sitting around the open fire, smoking, and looking very comfortable indeed. Before I was quite in the room they all stood up and began to praise the cake. I think Faye was the first to mention it, saying it was a "great success"; then the others said "perfectly delicious," and so on, but at the same time assuring me that a large piece had been left for me.

For one minute I stood still, not in the least grasping their meaning; but finally I suspected mischief, they all looked so serenely contented. So I passed on to the dining room, and there, on the table, was one of the precious cakes—at least what was left of it, the very small piece that had been so generously saved for me. And there were plates with crumbs, and napkins, that told the rest of the sad tale—and there was wine and empty glasses, also. Oh, yes! Their early Christmas had been a fine one. There was nothing for me to say or do—at least not just

then—so I went back to the little living-room and forced myself to be halfway pleasant to the four men who were there, each one looking precisely like the cat after it had eaten the canary! The cake was scarcely cold, and must have been horribly sticky—and I remember wondering, as I sat there, which one would need the doctor first, and what the doctor would do if they were all seized with cramps at the same time. But they were not ill—not in the least—which proved that the cake was well baked. If they had discovered the other one, however, there is no telling what might have happened.[12]

Ada A. Vogdes (left, above). Courtesy The Huntington Library, Art Collections, and Botanical Gardens.

Of course, not every frontier woman was a born cook. Ada A. Vogdes wrote of her frustrations in preparing the traditional Christmas turkey.

The elegant turkey, could he have seen himself after he was cook[ed] & ready for use, would have been ashamed of himself, could he have come to life suddenly. I did not know how to stuff him, or fill up those two hollows top and bottom, & his legs stuck straight up in the air, because I did not know where or how to fix them, & his wings had the expression as if he would like to take wing & flee away from such a scene. But he tasted just as well, as if his legs had been in a more proper shape & his wings had been pinned down to his side, but I must confess, without the stuffing in side he had rather a delapidated [sic] & collapsed appearance.

It is truly horrid to have more accomplishments than culinary knowledge.[13]

Imagine nearly ruining Christmas dinner because of military protocol! Civilian Anne E. Bingham recalled such a sight at Fort Leavenworth, Kansas, in 1869.

On Christmas day Captain Yates called to take my cousin and myself over to the soldiers' quarters to see their preparations for Christmas dinner. When we went in a soldier had just lifted the turkey from the oven to baste it. He had to stand at attention while an officer was in the room, and the contents of the pan on top of the stove sputtered and set the stove smoking with grease—all for army discipline.[14]

Notes

[1] Circular No. 56, Dec. 10, 1879, by order of Col. Albert G. Brackett, Fort Laramie, from the research files of Fort Laramie NHS.

[2] Katherine Gibson Fougera, *With Custer's Cavalry* (Caldwell, Ida.: The Caxton Printers, Ltd., 1942), 238.

[3] Douglas C. McChristian, ed., *Garrison Tangles in the Friendless Tenth: The Journal of First Lieutenant John Bigelow, Jr., Fort Davis, Texas* (Mattitack, N.Y.: J. M. Carroll & Company, 1985), 34-35.

[4] Bigelow, *On the Bloody Trail of Geronimo*, 100.

[5] John V. Lauderdale, Fort Bridger, to sister, Dec. 29, 1865, John Vance Lauderdale Collection, quoted courtesy Beinecke Rare Book and Manuscript Library, Western Americana Collection, Yale University.

[6] *Omaha Daily Bee,* Dec. 21, 1885.

[7] *ANJ,* Jan. 15, 1878.

[8] *ANR,* Jan. 4, 1882.

[9] Ibid., Jan. 26, 1884.

[10] Ibid., Jan. 8, 1887.

[11] Ibid., Dec. 26, 1891.

[12] Frances M. A. Roe, *Army Letters From An Officer's Wife, 1871-1888* (Lincoln: University of Nebraska Press, 1981), 24-26.

[13] Entry of Dec. 25, 1868, Journal of Ada A. Vogdes, 1868-71, quoted courtesy The Henry H. Huntington Library, San Marino, California.

[14] Anne E. Bingham, "Sixteen Years on a Kansas Farm, 1870-1886," *Collections of the Kansas State Historical Society, 1919-1922,* 15 (1923):503.

"Roasting the Christmas Beef in a Cavalry Camp." Engraving by Frederic Remington, *Harper's Weekly,* **Dec. 24, 1892.** Courtesy Frederic Remington Art Museum, Ogdensburg, New York.

1889 Merry Christmas 1889

Troop G, 1st U.S. Cavalry, Fort Custer, Montana

Soup, Oyster, Macaroni,
Broiled Prairie Chicken
Roast
Porterhouse Beef, Natural Sauce
Venison, Apple Sauce, Pig
Turkey, Cranberry Sauce
Oyster Dressing

Salads
Lobster, French Slaw, Shrimp

Vegetables
Potatoes, mashed   Onions, stewed
Sugar Corn   Beets
Potatoes, roasted   Tomatoes, stewed

Relishes
Worcestershire Sauce, Chow Chow
French Mustard
Pickled Cucumbers   Pickled Onions

Pastry
Mince Pie, Cranberry Pie, Apple Pie

Dessert
Preserved Peaches, Preserved Pears
Apples, Raisins, Nuts
Tea   Coffee   Chocolate

Chapter Five

. . .AND DRINK

"Outfit all drunk."

The frontier army was a hard-bitten, hard-fighting, and hard-drinking outfit, it being equally true of both officers and enlisted men. Due to isolation and boredom, soldiers often partook of the alcoholic beverages available chiefly from post traders or sutlers, sometimes spending their entire pay on liquor. It might be said that battling alcoholism posed an even greater threat than fighting Indians. However, Christmas was one of the few times when one's superiors more or less ignored imbibing.

Washington Matthews's comments in his diary on Christmas 1868 at Fort Rice, Dakota Territory, showed that soldiers laid away Christmas supplies of liquor with the post sutler well in advance. This was tolerated—if somewhat cavalierly—by the officers and Post Surgeon Matthews, who would be faced with the task of repairing any resulting human wreckage.

> **Dec. 24 A number of enlisted Germans having formed a German Society at the post, their first entertainment was given this Christmas Eve. It consisted of songs & supper and the drinking of a weak, home-made beer. The officers of the Fort were all invited.**
>
> **Dec. 25 A Christmas celebrated chiefly by the amount of whiskey drank at the post. Soldiers having filed away whiskey orders and stored away the article itself for some time past in view of the approaching festival.[1]**

H. H. McConnell, a Texas cavalryman and a bit of a snob, drew a distinction between the celebratory habits of the Civil War volunteer and the frontier regular, as he saw service with both.

> **During the Christmas holidays drunkenness was prevalent, and desertions very numerous, and I began to have an insight into the thousand and one ways and means that a solider will indulge in to get whiskey. Of course I had seen all these things, or most of them, during the war, but a volunteer soldier, even after three years active campaigning, finds himself a novice in all things pertaining to real army life when he "joins" the "regulars," and "gets onto" the devices of "sure enough" soldiers in time of peace.[2]**

Dr. Valentine T. McGillycuddy. NSHS-I392:15-1.

Fanny McGillycuddy, the young wife of army contract physician and later famous Indian agent Dr. Valentine T. McGillycuddy, commented succinctly on drunkenness at Camp Robinson, Nebraska, several days after the 1876 holiday.

Dec. 28th to 31st Very busy getting paper work done for hospital. Outfit all drunk.[3]

James Cunningham, an observer at Fort McDowell, Arizona Territory, reported an explosive Christmas holiday in 1874.

At six o'clock the ball-room was opened and dancing commenced. Irish jigs, Yankee breakdowns and Dutch waltzes were executed in good style, until eleven o'clock, when order, for a song, was demanded by the floor manager, and all resumed their seats. Several national, comic and sentimental songs were sung, which gave general satisfaction. Several kegs of beer were tapped and demolished, with some of the post trader's whisky. Numerous healths were proposed, which were responded to with repeated cheers, viz: "General Crook and lady;" "Captain Corliss and lady;" "Major Wells and lady;" also, "Lieutenant Carter," who, I am sorry to state, is about to leave us, much to the regret of his Company, in which he is much esteemed.

At three o'clock, there was a great sensation in the ball-room, by the explosion of a keg of lager, which was a great drawback to the proceedings—it being the only one left.

Dancing was kept up until five o'clock, when all returned to their quarters, and at reveille each man was at his place in the ranks, sober and able to perform anything imposed upon him. Such is the character of Co. C, 8th Infantry, and always has been with few exceptions, and will be for time to come.[4]

No exploding kegs of lager intruded on Lt. John G. Bourke's 1882 Christmas Eve dinner at Whipple Barracks, Arizona Territory, as his gourmand's description pretentiously attested.

> **December 24th, 1882. Christmas Eve. The Bachelor's Mess celebrated Christmas with a very enjoyable & well-cooked dinner, admirably served under the superintendence of our efficient landlady, Mrs. DeWitt.**
>
> **Nearly everything on the bill of fare had been brought by Rail from Los Angeles, Cal. to Manicopa Wells, Arizona and thence hauled in wagons to Prescott.**
>
> **The oranges, apples, almonds and raisins—all of California growth—were equal to anything of the kind imported, while the wines—sherry and claret—from the same land of Angels—were gratifying assurances that America is soon to throw off the yoke of dependence in the matter of table beverages.**
>
> **The sherry—of great alcoholic strength and fine bouquet—has a somewhat unpleasant, earthy after-taste, but the claret, rich, fruity, finely flavored and of good body, is superior to the best of France.[5]**

"One for the road" was hardly an uncommon occurrence, but as noted in this anonymous reminiscence, there was a price to pay.

> **It was Christmas eve, 1890, at Fort Douglas, Salt Lake City, where the old Sixteenth was stationed, when we got orders to move up. The boys had started on a round of holiday carousing, and tom-and-jerry bowls were being emptied faster than they could be filled to the tune of maudlin songs. Consequently, when our troop train pulled out for Cheyenne before daybreak, it was a bleary-eyed mob, entirely lacking in the Christmas spirit of peace on earth and good will, that huddled in shivering groups on the flat cars.[6]**

Frederic Remington, the well-known western artist, was also a keen observer and writer. Camped with a group of soldiers in South Dakota in 1890, Remington sketched a picture and wrote about the frigid Christmas night he spent in a Sibley tent.

> **"Eat, drink, and be merry, for to-morrow we die." Not a good excuse, but it has been sufficient on many occasions to be true. The soldier on campaign passes life easily. He holds it in no strong grip, and the Merry Christmas evening is as liable to be spent in the saddle in fierce contact with a blizzard as in his cosey tepee with his comrades and his scant cheer. The jug containing the spirits of the occasion may have**

"A Merry Christmas in a Sibley Tent." Engraving by Frederic Remington, *Harper's Weekly,* **Dec. 5, 1891.** Courtesy Frederic Remington Art Museum, Ogdensburg, New York.

been gotten from a town fifty miles away on the railroad. It is certainly not the distillation of the summer sunlight, and it is probably "tough" enough stuff to mingle naturally with his surroundings; but if one "drinks no more than a sponge" he may not have the jaded, retrospective feeling and the moral mending on the day to come. To sit on a camp chest, and to try to forget that the soldier's quart cup is not filled with the best in the market, and then to enter into the full appreciation of the picturesque occasion, is to forget that long marches, "bull meat," and sleepless, freezing nights are in the background. Pleasant hours sit so nicely in their complemental surrounding of hard ones, since everything in the world is relative. As to the eating in a cavalry camp on campaign, it is not overdone, for beans and coffee and bacon and bacon and coffee and beans come round with sufficient regularity to forestall all gormandizing. The drinking is not the prominent feature either, but helps to soften the asperities of a Dakota blizzard which is raging on the other side of the "ducking."

The Sibley tent weaves and moans and tugs frantically at its pegs. The Sibley stove sighs like a furnace while the cruel wind seeks out the holes and crevices. The soldiers sit in their camp drawing-room buttoned up to the chin in their big

canvas overcoats, and the muskrat caps are not removed. The freemasonry of the army makes strong friendships, and soldiers are all good fellows, that being part of their business. There are just enough exceptions to prove the rule. The cold, bloodless, compound-interest snarler is not in the army, and if he were he would be as cheerless on a damp evening as he would in a fight. One man is from Arizona, another from Washington, and the rest from the other corners of Uncle Sam's tract of land. They have met before, and memory after memory comes up with its laughter and pathos of the old campaigns. One by one the "shoulder straps" crawl in through the hole in the tepee. And, mind you, they do not walk in like a stage hero, with dash and abandon and head in the air; they prostrate themselves like a Turk at prayer, and come crawling. If they raise the flap ever so much, and bring company of the Dakota winds, they are met with a howl of protests. After gaining erectness, they brush the snow from their clothes, borrow a tin cup, and say, "How! how!"[7]

Drinking, at times, produced an entertaining mixture of the comic and the near tragic. Lydia Spencer Lane, wife of 1st Lt. William Bartlett Lane, a mounted rifleman stationed at Fort Clark in antebellum Texas, recalled a hazardous Christmas day journey in 1855—hazardous due to her driver's intoxication.

The day before Christmas we left Fort Clark for a second visit to San Antonio and Austin. The weather was like summer, and the evening was so warm in camp we were glad to get out of the tent for the air. By morning a stiff norther was blowing, and water in a bucket in the tent froze to the bottom. It was bitter cold, and we were so anxious about the baby, fearing she might freeze to death. Our ambulance was better calculated for a summer ride than a journey on a freezing winter's day. Our driver, Biles by name, had begun very early in the morning to celebrate Christmas by taking a great deal more whiskey than was good for him, which he procured from some unknown source. As it was a warm day when we left Fort Clark, he, soldier-like, "took no thought for the morrow," and forgot his overcoat. We found out as soon as we started from camp that the man was too drunk to drive, and we had not gone far before he became unconscious. He was propped up on the front seat beside husband, who drove, and who occasionally administered a sharp crack over his head with the whip, to rouse him and keep him from freezing

to death. I sat behind, with the baby on my lap, completely covered with blankets to protect her from the wind, and many an anxious peep I took to see how she fared, lest, while keeping her warm and excluding the cold air, I might smother her.

There we were, travelling over the prairie, far from any settlement, with no escort, and a young baby and a helplessly drunken soldier to be cared for. It was an anxious day for us, and we were much relieved when, late in the afternoon, we could see the little town of Dhanis in the distance, where we would find a fire and the assistance we needed.[8]

Some frontier army wives were not above joining in the imbibing. Ada A. Vogdes, wife of Lt. Anthony W. Vogdes, recounts such a story from Fort Laramie in 1868. Her frankness is refreshing.

Christmas I drank so many different kinds of liquor, that I retired quite up side down to my couch, and although I was perfectly still, & quiet myself, the bed, & things around, would roll, & keep in perpetual motion. I think my brain had St. Vituses [Vitus's] dance.[9]

Artillery Punch

1/4 lb. good green tea	3 qts. Catawba wine
1 qt. St. Croix rum	1 qt. brandy
1 qt. rye whiskey	1 qt. gin
1-1/4 lb. brown sugar	1 pt. preserved cherries
9 oranges	9 lemons

Put the tea into 1/2 gallon cold water overnight. Strain, and add juice or oranges and lemons. Add brown sugar, cherries, and all liquors. Cover lightly and allow to stand for from two to six weeks. (There is honest difference of opinion as to whether a stone crock or cedar tub makes the best container.) To serve, mix one gallon of the liquid with one gallon of champagne, and pour over a large piece of ice in punch bowl. Researchers must be warned that tasting the liquid prior to mixing and serving results in a high casualty rate. Under field conditions, a modified formula (much, in fact, like the ancestral form), served from a bucket, proved a potent brave-maker.

From *Military Collector & Historian: Journal of The Company of Military Historians.*

Others in the military family resisted the temptation of libations and made sure that others knew of their teetotalling ways. Dr. John V. Lauderdale, a Fort Bridger surgeon, wrote to his sister in 1865:

> **Saturday Evening. I have not told you how I spent christmas day. All of the officers were invited to the Judges about 1 P.M. to partake of a preliminary collation consisting of egg nog, cake, apples, and fruit and nuts. All of which was very fine. They said the nog was good but my teetotalism would not allow me to verify the fact.**[10]

Catharine Wever Collins, wife of Col. William O. Collins, commander of the Eleventh Ohio Volunteer Cavalry at Fort Laramie, also refused eggnog at an 1863 party.

> **While I have been away John baked the bread that I made up and has made and is now baking some cake. I hope it will prove good as we wish some day next week to have a reception or something of the kind. We have another invitation for this evening for cake and egg-nog at Mr. [William G.] Bullock's. I told Mr. B. I would call and take some cake if he would excuse me about the egg-nogg [sic].**[11]

Lt. John Bigelow recounted—with some disgust—the unavailability of one soldier to attend a holiday dinner at Fort Davis, Texas, in 1884.

> **I was mortified that Hughes (Lieut.) was prevented from attending through temporary indisposition, consequent upon too much punch drinking in the course of the forenoon. I did not like Clarke's off hand way of appologizing [sic] for his absence: "He is not well. You will have to excuse him." I doubt very much whether Mrs. Ayres did excuse him.**[12]

Lt. Alexander R. Piper, Eighth Infantry, left Fort Robinson for Pine Ridge Agency, South Dakota, in December 1890. Piper tried his best to avoid the alcoholic temptations all around him.

> **Last night, Squires of the 7th gave a big blowout, a fine lunch and lots of punch. I expected it would be a big drunk so did not go down. In the 2nd Infantry Camp one crowd had punch and another egg-nog. I also steered clear of those tents. About nine o'clock Bookmiller brought me a cup of punch.**[13]

Temperance organizations made an appearance at many posts in an attempt to dissuade drinking. In a seeming contradiction Eveline M. Alexander, wife of Maj. Andrew J. Alexander, Eighth Cavalry, enjoyed the decorations sponsored

Egg Nog

4 egg yolks
4 Tbsps. sugar
1 cup cream (whipping)
1 cup brandy
1/4 cup wine
4 egg whites
a little grated nutmeg

Beat the egg yolks until light; then slowly beat in the sugar, cream, brandy and wine. Whip the egg whites separately, and then fold into the other ingredients. Sprinkle with nutmeg to serve.

Recipe from *The Civil War Cookbook* by William C. Davis.

by the Sons of Temperance at Fort Union, New Mexico, for Christmas 1866—followed by a holiday eggnog at home!

In the morning went to church with Andrew. Mr. Morte has arranged a very nice little chapel here in the building of the Sons of Temperance. It was very prettily trimmed with greens and looked really like Christmas.

On our return from church I had all the noncommissioned officers of G Company to take eggnog and lunch with us. A sort of farewell to G Company. It passed off very successfully.[14]

Not all of Elizabeth's Custer's memories during her long widowhood were painful. To her, we owe many of the best frontier army memories and tales of day-to-day existence. They include the following piece of hilarity from an unidentified Kansas location, between a put upon quartermaster and a tipsy "Judy O'Grady" from the laundress line.

There was joy in garrison one morning when a little tale of what we considered a case of justice meted out came travelling along from one woman to another. It was Christmas morning, and though there were no chimes to ring us up, no carols to delight our ears, we felt convivial even over the extra nap with which we celebrated the day. The quartermaster, sleeping in his comfortable bed, was called out in the gray of early dawn, that coldest chill, just before daybreak, striking him as he went barefooted through his hall, while his heart was beating with alarm for fear of disaster or fire, as he answered the bell. "Glad he was punished for having a bell when we had none," we said, savagely, when we heard this.

Elizabeth Custer. NSHS-B621.

On opening the door a dishevelled tipsy Jezebel of a camp-woman, bracing herself against the wood-work as best she could, said to him, "It's cold, and my nose bleeds," and with this informa-tion she departed. The woman who clamored for paint, another who ap-pealed in vain for necessary repairs, had no compunc-tions in laughing at this case of woman's inhumanity to man, and if we suffered for anything after that, we summed up every misery with the words, "It's cold, and my nose bleeds."[15]

Notes

[1] Ray H. Mattison, ed., "The Diary of Surgeon Washington Matthews, Fort Rice, D.T." *North Dakota History* 21 (Jan.-Apr., 1954):28-29.

[2] H. H. McConnell, *Five Years a Cavalryman; or, Sketches of Regular Army Life on the Texas Frontier, Twenty Odd Years Ago* (Freeport, N.Y.: Books for Libraries Press, 1970), 42.

[3] "Exact Copy of a Notebook Kept by Dr. V. T. McGillycuddy, M.D., while a Member of the Yellowstone and Big Horn Expedition, May 26-Dec. 13, 1876, and Notes Kept by His Wife, Fanny, at Camp Robinson, Dec. 13, 1876-Feb.22, 1877," copy on file at the Fort Robinson Museum, Crawford, Nebraska.

[4] *Arizona Miner* (Prescott), Jan. 8, 1875.

[5] Bourke diary, no. 63, 1882.

[6] Undated clipping, source unknown.

[7] "A Merry Christmas in a Sibley Tent," *Harper's Weekly,* Dec. 5, 1891; reprinted in Frederic Remington, *Pony Tracks* (Norman: University of Oklahoma Press, 1961), 157-60.

[8] Lydia Spencer Lane, *I Married a Soldier* (Albuquerque: University of New Mexico Press, 1987), 39-40.

[9] Entry of Dec. 27, 1868, Journal of Ada A. Vogdes.

[10] Lauderdale to sister, Dec. 29, 1865, Lauderdale Collection.

[11] Agnes Wright Spring, ed., "An Army Wife Comes West: Letters of Catharine Wever Collins (1863-1864)," *The Colorado Magazine* 31 (Oct. 1954):253.

[12] McChristian, *Garrison Tangles,* 35.

[13] John M. Carroll, ed. "Extracts from Letters Written by Lieutenant Alexander R. Piper, 8th Infantry, at Pine Ridge Agency, South Dakota, to His Wife, Marie Cozzens Piper, at Fort Robinson, Nebraska, during the Sioux Campaign, 1890-1891," *The Unpublished Papers of the Order of Indian Wars, Book #10* (New Brunswick, N.J.: Privately published, 1977):4.

[14] Sandra L. Myres, ed., *Cavalry Wife: The Diary of Eveline M. Alexander, 1866-1867* (College Station: Texas A&M University Press, 1977), 113.

[15] Eizabeth B. Custer, *Following the Guidon* (Lincoln: University of Nebraska Press, 1994), 228-29.

Chapter Six

DECORATIONS

"Not a green branch or twig in the entire country."

The traditional Victorian style of decorating, the motto of which might be "more is marvelous," did not come easily for those living on frontier army posts. Lack of resources, both financial and natural, made it difficult to capture the Christmas spirit. However, even those stationed in the most remote regions—posts where not a green tree could be found—did their best to make the holiday special.

The most popular decoration, then as now, was the Christmas tree, by all accounts introduced to America by Hessians during the Revolutionary War. Prince Albert's gift of a tree to Queen Victoria in England, and the subsequent publicity in American newspapers and popular magazines, did much for its gain in popularity in the last half of the 1800s.

The Victorians decorated their trees differently than we do ours. They started out using small trees, which were displayed upon table tops.

Eventually, larger trees became more common. Trees displayed a wide array of decorations, usually all hand-made. Magazines of the day, such as *Godey's Lady's Book*, were full of decorating ideas and instructions. (Commercially made ornaments were not widely available until the 1880s.) Strings of popcorn, cranberries, paper cornucopias, bouquets of paper flowers, bows, lace bags filled with candy, and streamers were common ornamentations. Small candles provided illumination. Lighting of the tree was a special occasion, usually done only once or twice and always with a well-placed bucket of water on hand. (The first electrified tree appeared in New York in 1882, the first commercially sold electric tree lights sometime in the 1890s.) In addition, gifts served as ornaments for the tree. Small items, such as mittens, pin cushions, and dolls, hung from the branches until it was time for them to be distributed to the lucky recipients.

Emily McCorkle FitzGerald. From *An Army Doctor's Wife on the Frontier* by Emily FitzGerald, © 1962 by University of Pittsburgh Press. Reprinted by permission of the University of Pittsburgh Press.

Emily McCorkle FitzGerald, stationed with her husband, Dr. Jenkins A. FitzGerald, at Fort Sitka, a remote Alaska post, told of her family's hand-made 1875 Christmas.

Christmas is over and the steamer that was to have taken this letter has not yet arrived. It is too mean we had to have our Christmas without it. . . .

Our Christmas passed off very pleasantly. We lighted up our tree, as we intended, on the afternoon before, and we had all the babies here together. Indeed, the whole garrison was here, but my tree was particularly the babies' tree. Doctor is so nice about such things. He took such pains with the tree and such an interest in it on the children's account. I had pretty little presents for them all, at least all except the little babies, as the rubber toys for them have not arrived. You would be surprised to see how many little things we got up out of nothing—little bits of ribbon and bright cardboard and little pictures, etc. Then Doctor made me some of the cutest rustic frames with his saw, and I framed some little gem chromos. I had two or three neckties I found I could spare and, as we were short of Christmas gifts, I made use of those. You can't imagine how pretty they look on a tree, tucked up in loops

In 1896 the ballroom at Fort Wingate, New Mexico, was decorated with patriotic finery for Troop E, Second Cavalry. Photo by Ben Wittick. Courtesy Museum of New Mexico, neg. no. 39377.

and just drawn under a round, scalloped paper. They look like bouquets; a pink one looks like a great rose. It was my own idea, and I am quite delighted with it, as everyone admired it. Indeed I am feeling quite accomplished in getting up things. I made some lovely big stars to ornament my tree by cutting stars out of cardboard and covering both sides with sheet lead, then pinching it down at the edges to make it hold. Doctor made candlesticks and got just the loveliest tree in the neighborhood. It stood on the floor and the first limbs came out just over Bessie's head. The trunk was wrapped with green and Bess's little dishes were set out on a little table under it. That pleased the children awfully, and they had a tea party under the tree while we big folks ate cake and talked. Bertie ate the spout off the tea pot! The tree, when lighted up, did look pretty, and I always mean to have one.

Then on Christmas night (last night) Mrs. Campbell had all the big folks over there and her tree was ever so pretty, too. She had almost as much contrivance as I had, but her sister had sent her a whole big box of decorations—all sorts of bright things and the prettiest little banners I ever saw made out of some transparent stuff with "Merry Christmas" on them. We had a real merry evening. . . .In talking of decorating the trees, I forgot to say rock candy is so pretty. Get it in long, thin sticks. It looks and sparkles like icicles.[1]

Julia Gilliss was stationed with her husband Capt. James Gilliss of the Quartermaster Department at Fort Stevens, Oregon, for Christmas 1866. She wrote in a letter to her sister of wanting to be back home to decorate the family tree. Interestingly, she notes that she has some items available to her for decorations that she had not had in the past.

> **I suppose this will reach you about Christmas, so I hope you will all be merry and happy. I wish that I was with you to dress the Christmas tree. I've got such nice little pictures & ribbons etc. to make cornucopias. . . .You know how much trouble we had to get the right kind when we trimmed the last tree when I was home.[2]**

Fanny Corbusier, wife of army surgeon William H. Corbusier, stationed at Camp McDermit, Nevada, for Christmas 1873, made her own tree, which did not seem to lessen its impact on one bright-eyed child.

> **We took Claude in to see the tree which was a very small one, simply some willow branches for which I made leaves out of green paper. It was decorated with cranberries, popcorn, candles and candy. A little boy, one of a couple, who lived near the Post, came early about four o'clock, as he did not**  **want to miss seeing Santa Claus. The latter arrived about six-thirty p.m. shaking his bells. The little fellow, who was about nine years old, had never seen Santa Claus or a Christmas tree before. It was sweet to see his enjoyment. When he was leaving I wrapped up his presents and candy and cake and handed them to him. "Oh," he said, "I don't deserve all that, I have had such a good time." He didn't want to take the things; he had no idea what Christmas meant. He was not poor, as his father had plenty, but they were so far away from all such things and it may be they had no memories of Christmases past to tell their little son about.[3]**

Caroline Frey Winne wrote of her efforts to gather items to decorate her windswept quarters of Fort McPherson, Nebraska, in 1877.

> **Mrs. Carr has promised to take me out into one of the canyons to get cedar & bittersweet berries to trim the house for Christmas. So far as climate & country is concerned, we have gained by coming here. But for all, I do want to come home, more than I can tell anybody.[4]**

Katherine Gibson, wife of Capt. Francis M. Gibson, Seventh Cavalry, recalled that, while some items were available for an upcoming Christmas tree party they planned to host, there was not a tree to be found at Fort Abraham Lincoln, Dakota Territory, 1875.

> **With the approach of roaring December my husband and I decided to give a Christmas tree party at our quarters on Christmas Eve, but where to find either tree or trimmings was the problem. The trader's store offered a meager assortment of articles, and the commissary could supply only such**

Homemade decorations brightened the Seventh Battery's Christmas dinner at Fort Riley in 1904. Courtesy Joseph J. Pennell Collection, Kansas Collection, University of Kansas Libraries.

staples as sugar, coffee, flour, and other simple necessities. However, soldiers were sent out to scour the neighborhood for anything that looked like a tree and finally returned with some forlorn bunches of squatty sage and cedar brush. The outlook was discouraging, but it stimulated imagination, and we started to fashion something that at least resembled a tree. We hung the plants in relays from the ceiling down to within a few feet of the floor, and beneath them was placed a wash-tub decorated with gaily painted paper and filled with sand and whatever crude presents the town of Bismarck afforded. A sort of Christmas pie idea. So far so good, but now for the trimmings, and in this paper played the most conspicuous part. Paints were produced and brushes wielded, while plain paper took on startling colors, and scissors were busy cutting yards and yards into strips, which served as festoons or were converted into cornucopias to be filled with homemade candy. Some thrifty soul had garnered a few nuts and these were dexterously covered with silver foil salvaged from cigars and then hung upon the tree along with ancient Christmas cards, resurrected from trunks, and tied with scraps of faded ribbon which had been ironed and freshened.

Jack Sturgis and some other youngsters just out of the Point displayed hidden artistic talents. They colored candles bright red, cut them in two, and perched them jauntily on the branches. They fashioned a huge paper bell, also painted red, pasting on the edges cut-out pictures of Santa Claus, and when the work was completed the ensemble stood forth as a thing of beauty.[5]

In 1872 the residents of Camp Hancock, Dakota Territory, faced a similar dearth of suitable trees and came up with a unique idea, witnessed by Linda W. Slaughter.

Thirty years ago in 1872 I spent Christmas at Camp Hancock. The buildings were the same as today, one story, hewed log houses, that have since been raised and remodeled. The two sets of officers' quarters were occupied by Capt. E. E. Clarke, post commandant, and Dr. B. F. Slaughter, post surgeon, the two lieutenants, Humbert and Chance, being absent on leave of absence. The building nearest the street was the surgeon's quarters, and we had a Christmas tree there on Christmas eve, just thirty years ago, the first in Bismarck. The children of this modern Bismarck will no doubt think it a funny tree. I had taught a little Sunday school of the chil-

dren of Edwinton all summer in my tent at Camp Hancock, and when Christmas came and I had the luxury of living in a real house, of course, the Sunday school scholars must have a Christmas tree. But what should it be made of? Not a green branch or twig in the entire country. But we had a Christmas tree, notwithstanding. Dr. Slaughter possessed a pair of magnificent elk horns of which he was very proud, and we had the post carpenter fasten them upright in the center of the dining room, and decked them up with pretty ribbons and bright colored fringes and fastened little gifts to its many prongs and supplemented it with a treat made up of all the "goodies" the commissary and village stores could furnish. There were eleven happy little boys and girls at that Christmas tree gathering, and they sang "I Want to be an Angel" and "Happy Land" and listened to the "Old, Old Story," that Sunday school children in Bismarck hear today. Then we played games until bedtime, and they were sent home happy.[6]

The company mess hall might naturally shine in the martial splendor of flag, drum, guidon, and highly polished brass, but often a feminine hand with green paper softened it with wreaths and garlands. A correspondent from Fort McKinney, Wyoming, reported on their Christmas celebration to the readers of the *Army and Navy Register* in 1890.

Although a little late for Christmas news, still a few words regarding our holiday season may prove interesting. Never during our sojourn here has the true Yule tide feeling made itself felt to a greater extent and all were willing victims to its influence. The festivities were inaugurated on Christmas Eve by a "doll's" tree, almost wholly the work of the small people of the post and to which all the little ones were invited regardless of race or color; it is needless to remark that unalloyed happiness reigned supreme. The troop and company dinners were the features of the great feast day itself. As "K," Twenty-first Infantry, Lieutenant Hearns commanding, dined at an unusually early hour, we cannot speak of the dinner itself from actual observation, but as the company rejoices in three professional bakers comment is unnecessary. At 2:30 o'clock the strength of the garrison, headed by our genial commanding officer and Mrs. Henry, filed from the officers' line and proceeded en masse to Troop D barrack, Captain Loud

commanding, where on entering the mess hall we were received with songs and music by the talent of the troop. The hall was elaborately decorated with greens and appropriate emblems, one of the most attractive being a gigantic menu card fully 3 x 2½ feet square, very kindly executed by the sister of our popular young adjutant. The tables were loaded to overflowing with all the delicacies of the season. After exhausting our vocabulary of praise our little party wended its way to Troop H, Captain Dimmick commanding, where we were received by its stalwart sergeant, who, in stentorian tones, gave the usual order "attention" as we entered the door. Here again elaborate decoration met our sight, the "Ship of State" composed almost entirely of pines being the most conspicuous; it was complete in every part, even to its piney anchor. Signs of welcome greeted us on every side, the tables fairly groaning under their burden of good things. Before leaving the quarters the health of its officers and men was drunk in sparkling champagne.[7]

James Cunningham, an observer at Camp McDowell, Arizona, shared with the editor of the *Arizona Miner* a description of the patriotic decorations for Christmas 1874.

> With feelings of pleasure, I hasten to give you a brief re-count of Christmas festivities in Company C, 8th Infantry, stationed at Camp McDowell.
>
> Through the extreme kindness of Captain Corliss and lady, all the delicacies that could be had within reach were pro-cured and cooked for the occasion, in exquisite style. The mess hall was decorated with national flags and wreaths of evergreen, under which were printed in large letters, "Hail Columbia," "Uphold the Flag," "Long may it wave." In the centre was suspended an eagle with both wings extended, as large as life, beautifully decorated, for which, great praise is due to Chas. Egan, post painter.[8]

Residents at Fort Fred Steele, Wyoming, used military accoutrements for decorations at Christmas 1885.

Fort Riley's Nineteenth Battery decorated its dining room in 1902 with sabers and bunting. Courtesy Joseph J. Pennell Collection, Kansas Collection, University of Kansas Libraries.

> Of the three companies of the 21st Infantry stationed here, B, I, and K, two, I and K, on their arrival were recently the recipients of courtesies at the hands of Co. B. It was deemed proper that some suitable return be made, and committees were appointed to at once to arrange the various details for a ball and supper to be given in honor of Co. B. on Christmas eve, Dec. 24. The use of an unoccupied company quarters was obtained for the purpose and the work begun. Fruits and other articles for the supper not to be had here were ordered from abroad. Juniper brush (the only kind of evergreen obtainable in this region) was brought in. The walls were festooned, and wreaths, each one surrounding an army corps

badge, to the number of sixteen, were given prominent places among the decorations. The entire hall was canopied with large flags, and from the centre of the ceiling was suspended a chandelier—kindly furnished by our post trader—above which was a star formed of bayonets.[9]

A more elaborate set of decorations became a source of pride and tradition at the well-known 1878 Memorial Chapel at Fort Leavenworth, Kansas. It remains an old army symbol and a revered shrine still in regular use. As reported in the *Leavenworth Times* in 1887, all looked forward to the tree in the post chapel and the related festivities.

Chaplain Barry and his efficient aides were busily engaged yesterday afternoon preparing a Christmas tree in the Post chapel. The tree is a very large evergreen of the pine species, and stands over thirty feet high. It is beautifully ornamented with novel and costly articles to attract the eye and make glad the hearts of the little ones as well as those of an older and larger growth. The decorations were completed last night as well as the placing thereon of presents also. The chapel will be open all day today, in order that all may avail themselves of an opportunity to see the largest and most finely decorated Christmas tree in Leavenworth. It is a sight well worth seeing, and those anxious to look at it should go today and avoid the rush which will be sure to take place tonight, as it is the intention to seat the Sunday school scholars first and the parents and people afterwards.

The exercises tonight will consist of singing of Christmas carols by the children and other music.

The chapel is very tastefully decorated with evergreens, wreaths, etc., and attracts universal attention.[10]

Notes

[1] Emily McCorkle FitzGerald, *An Army Doctor's Wife on the Frontier: The Letters of Emily McCorkle FitzGerald from Alaska and the Far West, 1874-1878,* Abe Laufe, ed. (Lincoln: University of Nebraska Press, 1986), 170-72.

[2] Julia Gilliss, *So Far From Home: An Army Bride on the Western Frontier, 1865-1869,* Priscilla Knuth, ed. (Portland: Oregon Historical Society Press, 1993), 105-6.

[3] Fanny Corbusier journal, quoted courtesy Nancy Corbusier Knox, Corbusier Archives, Santa Fe.

[4] Buecker, "Letters of Caroline Frey Winne," 41.

[5] Fougera, *With Custer's Cavalry,* 237-38.

[6] *Bismarck Tribune,* Dec. 24, 1902.

[7] *ANR,* Jan. 1, 1890.

[8] *Arizona Miner,* Jan. 8, 1875.

[9] *ANJ,* Jan. 9, 1886.

[10] *Leavenworth Times,* Dec. 24, 1887.

Chapter Seven

GIFTS

"There is not a dollie in town."

Nowhere did the frontier army wife show more inventiveness than in procuring Christmas gifts. Parents spared no effort for the children of the post. All children—regardless of the parent's rank—were treated equally when it came to Christmas gifts. It was the one time of the year when everyone at a post could come together for their benefit.

Once again, having a railroad nearby played a major role in gift giving and receiving. The best of the eastern stores were at the beck and call of anyone via a well-thumbed catalog. Advertisements for toys and trinkets of all kinds appeared in magazines and newspapers. For the isolated celebrant, though, there was the oft-repaired and remade. Making Christmas presents also served as a form of recreation.

In 1871 Frances M. A. Roe, as was customary, laid out all the gifts her family had received for

Santa left an abundance of toys at Lt. Alvarado M. Fuller's Fort Huachuca residence, 1894. Courtesy Fort Huachuca Museum.

display to the officers and wives at Fort Lyon, Colorado Territory. Concerned about what her peers might think when they saw no presents from her family back east, she came up with an ingenious solution.

Our first Christmas on the frontier was ever so pleasant, but it certainly was most vexatious not to have that box from home. And I expect that it has been at Kit Carson for days, waiting to be brought down. We had quite a little Christmas without it, however, for a number of things came from the girls, and several women of the garrison sent pretty little gifts to me. It was so kind and thoughtful of them to remember that I might be a bit homesick just now. All the little presents were spread out on a table, and in a way to make them present as fine an appearance as possible. Then I printed in large letters, on a piece of cardboard, "One box— contents unknown!" and stood it up on the back of the table. I did this to let everyone know that we had not been forgotten by home people. My beautiful new saddle was brought in, also, for although I had had it several weeks, it was really one of Faye's Christmas gifts to me.[1]

Of course transportation could not always be depended upon, even with plenty of advance planning. Mrs. Orsemus (Frances) Bronson Boyd recalled one young officer's wife's Christmas trials.

I remember being once consulted about a Christmas present designed for her husband. She had decided upon a beautiful picture, which, although ordered in ample time, did not arrive until long after the holidays, and the express charges alone were fifty dollars.[2]

Children were cherished in the frontier west. Childbirth and early infancy carried a high mortality rate, and the "usual childhood diseases" posed a particular terror. Even with the best of intentions, care, and compassion, the post surgeon had neither the training nor medications to be a skilled pediatrician. There was no defense against cholera and typhoid.

If a child survived these deadly diseases, the chances increased that he or she would grow into a sturdy, clear-eyed, fearless youngster. It is no small wonder then that much of an army Christmas focused on the young.

Forrestine Cooper Hooker, daughter of Lt. Charles L. Cooper, Tenth Cavalry, reminisced of Christmas 1872 at Fort Sill, Oklahoma. It speaks volumes of the lengths to which parents would go to please their children.

Christmas morning, 1872, is vividly impressed upon my memory, though I was not six years old until the following March. My brother Harry stood beside me at the closed door which led from the hallway into the living room of our quarters. My father opened the door and we gazed at our first real Christmas tree, decorated with things that had been sent from Philadelphia for this event. Under the tree were two tiny

folding chairs with wooden legs and arms of black, white canvas seats, and backs bound with red braid. In one chair was an immense wax doll in a red dress. That was my chair; the other was for my brother. Then I saw two strange objects on the mantel above the open fireplace. They had not been there when we hung up our stockings the previous night. One was a boy in French bisque holding a pole and a string of fish; at the other end of the mantel stood a girl with a net of fish. The statuettes were about fifteen inches high and tinted in colors.

At once I assumed that these were gifts to my brother and me, and I claimed the fisher girl, generously permitting my brother to own the boy. My parents explained to me that Mr. John Evans, the post trader, had sent the figurines as a Christmas gift to them, but I could call the fisher girl my own if I wanted to, and the boy could be called my brother's. From that day to this the two little French bisque figures have been a feature in my mother's home, and in various sections of the country the fisher boy and girl have stood as they did that Christmas morning of 1872, looking down on a crude little walnut tobacco box that Tom Custer had given to my father in 1870.

I sat in my new chair, selected by my father and mother from the articles displayed in the trader store of Mr. Evans, and held my doll in my arms. At that moment my mother carried my baby sister into the room and told me that I could hold her for a little while. The new sister, Florence, born on November 13, 1872, was not much larger than my wax doll.[3]

Emily McCorkle FitzGerald was stationed with her husband, Dr. Jenkins A. FitzGerald, at remote Fort Sitka, Alaska, in 1875. In a letter to her mother, FitzGerald proudly described her creativity in fashioning gifts for her daughter.

I have been busy for the last three or four days getting ready for Christmas. There is not a dollie in town. Everybody has been out looking for them. Bess is short of dollies. . . .

Mrs. Field and Mrs. Smith both had been looking for dollies to give Bess and had not found any. So I got the trunks of two of the dollies that had China hands and legs, and I made rag legs and arms for them and mended up two broken heads. I am going to dress them brightly and have a little table set with the little dishes and dollies taking breakfast at it on Christmas morning.[4]

Two years later in 1877 FitzGerald, now stationed at Fort Boise, asked her mother to send some things from back east, which led to a celebration little different than that of a well-to-do family in more settled regions. After a few lean years, the FitzGerald family celebrated the holiday a little more extravagantly.

I think it about time for me to acknowledge the receipt of some of the nice bundles that have come to us from Chestnut Hill in the last week. Your letter came on Friday, and the bundles for Bess and Bert on Saturday, and the children have felt very rich in Christmas gifts. They were all just as nice as they could be. Bess was charmed with the dollie, and the shoes to come off nearly set her wild. We wanted the acrobats for Bertie, and I am glad you sent them. He plays with them a great deal. His Papa makes him all sorts of new combinations not on the list. The animals and magnetic toys were entirely new to the children, and they enjoy them ever so much. The books are too nice for common, and after putting them in their playhouses with all the rest for Christmas morning, I brought them to my bookshelves, in the sitting room, and only mean them for the evenings and Sundays.

Bessie FitzGerald and her Christmas dollie. From *An Army Doctor's Wife on the Frontier* by Emily FitzGerald, © 1962 by University of Pittsburgh Press. Reprinted by permission of the University of Pittsburgh Press.

I think, Mamma, the pin from you is beautiful. Doctor says he has not seen anything he liked so much for a long time. His handkerchief, too, he says, is the nicest one he has ever had, and we both are just as much pleased and obliged as we could possibly be. So many pretty things all coming at once nearly sets me beside myself.

I hope you had a lovely Christmas. We had a quiet one, but a very pleasant one. The children had a delightful one. They had a tree, trimmed up with what was left from last year, and Doctor made them each a playhouse. He got Bert a big wagon and Bess a trunk. Then I had a lot of little things for them, and we turned one of the upstairs rooms into a play room and had all their toys together. They had, and are having still, a very happy time.[5]

In 1885 the Post Chapel at Fort Leavenworth, Kansas, was again the site of a special Christmas Eve celebration especially for the children of the post.

"This happy day, whose then sun
Shall set not through eternity,
This holy day when Christ the Lord,
Took on Him our humanity,
For little children everywhere
A joyous season still we make
We bring our precious gifts to them
E'en for the dear child Jesus' sake."

A genuine Christmas eve was that which was witnessed in the post chapel at Fort Leavenworth last night. The weather outside was anything but what it should be on Christmas eve. The chapel and its decorations were just what they should be on such a hallowed occasion.

On all its walls, in and around the many tables thereon placed, festoons of evergreens could be seen hanging gracefully, with here and there a wreath of the same material. The chandelier in the center of the chapel was covered with mistletoe. On a large platform in the chancel stood the biggest Christmas tree the writer ever saw, and he has seen a great many. It was loaded with presents and beautifully trimmed, showing much taste and much care on the part of the committee having the matter in charge.

Every child on the [military] reservation was invited and 254 responded. Each one received a select orange, a box of candy and a very nice present. These articles were purchased by voluntary contributions from the people resident at Ft. Leavenworth and with the proceeds of the children's entertainment given at the hop room a short time since. The middle block of pews were reserved for the children. When they were seated the fathers and mothers that could be accommodated took seats, and then there was a large number left standing. At 7 o'clock the exercises began by one hundred trained children led by Messrs. Beach, Hays and Wills, Mrs. Babcock presiding at the organ, singing Christmas carols. Santa Claus then made his appearance. He was a little late because of the unfavorable weather outside, but he was as cordially received as though he had been on time. Then came the distribution of presents. Each little boy and girl came forward as his or her name was called and received the orange, the candy and the present intended for them. It was a

touchingly beautiful sight. The child of the officer and the child of the soldier were treated exactly alike. A noticeable feature of this Christmas gathering was the number of non-commissioned officers and soldiers that were present. There is no rank in religion, and there isn't any in the chapel at Fort Leavenworth. The men were very deferential and respectful, knew their place and kept it, but all the same they felt that they were in God's house, to celebrate the anniversary of the birth of his son, who in his life and death made possible the fatherhood of God and the brotherhood of man. The human soul bears no insignia of rank. . . .A large number of officers and ladies were present and contemplated the interesting scene with pleasure, a great many of them having contributed most bounteously to the children's entertainment. The distribution lasted about an hour, and the tired and happy children went home.[6]

A correspondent to the *Army and Navy Journal* wrote about the great joy and cleverness of Christmas Eve at Fort Coeur d'Alene, Idaho, in 1880. Again, the festivities centered around the children of the post.

> Christmas Eve found the people of Fort Coeur d'Alene congregated in their theatre, an unoccupied set of barracks, neatly fitted up and dedicated to them by their genial regi-

mental post quartermaster, Capt. Clark. Thither they had repaired, some to take part in and others to witness the undressing of a Christmas tree which had been dressed with beautiful and costly gifts purchased by the officers and ladies of the post for distribution among the children of "Slab Town," or "Laundresses Row." The tree being lighted and everything ready for their reception, the children, fifty in number, were marshalled into the theatre. Amy Wheaton and Annie Clark being at the head of the column, and Mrs. Clark and Mrs. Waring bringing up the rear as "file closers," organ playing and children singing. Reaching the tree, they executed the "Rally by Company," the tree being the "Centre skirmisher," and stood for a few moments admiring the elegant display before them, when suddenly their attention was diverted by an almost magical appearance upon the scene of a Santa Claus in the person of Lieut. Mallory, who was so bedecked with "hoary hair and beard," as to render recognition impossible. The unlooked for appearance of Santa Claus caused the children to scream—some with delight, others with fear. However, their wonder was soon turned to admiration, for Santa Claus immediately commenced his work of distribution, and in a short time every little arm was loaded with presents, and each little heart filled with delight. This more than praiseworthy idea of providing Christmas gifts for the children of the enlisted men of the post was first set upon foot by Mrs. Wheaton, though ably seconded by all the other ladies. As the last note of the closing hymn was heard, a heartfelt "God bless Mrs. Wheaton and the ladies" arose to the lips of every mother present, and was sincerely echoed by all who had witnessed the effect of her generous forethought.[7]

The children at Fort Hays, Kansas, were much beloved as well. A spectator at the post's festivities in 1888 wrote in glowing terms of the time and effort put into giving each child a special gift.

Probably the most enjoyable time ever experienced by the children of Fort Hays was from 6 to 8 o'clock Christmas eve.

It had been whispered for several days that Colonel and Mrs. Yard were "going to have a Christmas tree," but Madam Rumor could give no information whatever of how, when or where it was to be seen, or who were to be the recipients of the Christmas gifts.

On the morning of the 24th invitations were sent to the heads of families to come to the South Ward at the Post Hospital, at 6 p.m. sharp, and to "bring the children."

At the hour appointed all were there and many were the exclamations of delight from the children as they feasted their eyes upon the gorgeous scene presented by the magnificent Christmas tree illuminated with hundreds of wax candles.

After appropriate music rendered by a select orchestra of fine instruments played by members of the 18th Infantry Band, Old Santa Claus himself appeared upon the scene and took an active part for more than an hour in distributing the various gifts.

Mrs. Col. Yard, assisted by her charming daughter, Miss Annie, had with infinite pains selected presents adapted to the age and disposition of each and every child.

First Lieutenant George L. Turner, Adjutant 18th Infantry, was unable to be present, but he remembered each child of the Post School, of which he is the officer in charge, by presenting each with a handsomely bound book suited to the age of the recipient.

Miss Annie Yard presented each of the scholars with a souvenir in the shape of a beautiful hand-painted Christmas card appropriately inscribed.

Mr. Dillon, the Post school teacher, had a pleasant treat for his scholars in the way of sweet-meats and bon-bons.

Santa Claus kept calling the children up repeatedly; each time adding to their store of presents until they could no longer hold the many gifts in their arms and hands. . . .

At the close of the exercises the children pressed forward to thank Mrs. Colonel Yard for her generosity and kindness in their behalf, but she, anticipating them, had quietly left the room a few moments before, so at the time they could only thank her in their hearts for having made this one of the happiest days of their lives.[8]

Capt. Simon Snyder, Fifth Infantry, recalled in an 1879 diary entry his daughter's excitement over her presents.

Christmas day. Lillie woke this a.m. to find her dear little heart made glad by the gifts of Santa Claus. I do not think she expected much but she found a very pretty tree, a stocking full of candy and a handsome wax doll in another besides a number of presents for her little friends, all of which she delivered soon after breakfast.[9]

Caroline Frey Winne's accounting of Christmas 1879, at Fort Washakie, Wyoming Territory, also demonstrated the extravagance with which the holiday could be celebrated with gifts, particularly for their beloved son, nicknamed Bopper.

Charlie and I have come to the conclusion that we are glad Xmas comes once a year. for it has been a lively day I tell you. Bopper was loaded with presents, so many that he had no idea what to do with them all. he flitted about like a bird from one thing to another till he was tired out and his parents too except that I insisted upon his usual noon day nap he would have been tired out to death.

Mrs. Thomas had a tree last night for Georgie and invited all the children. It was to be lighted at five o'clock and baby was to go of course—when yesterday morning her baby broke out with measles so of course he couldn't go and didn't remember anything about its having been promised him. until this afternoon when I was drawing him on the porch— he saw some evergreens up by their house and he looked up at me with such a disappointed look and insisted upon going at once. I had to bring him in to divert him from it.

. . .The little boy has talked a great deal about Santa Claus coming down the chimney to fill his stocking and was very much interested & amused when I brought out a pair of little red stockings & pinned them up over the fire-place. This morning he woke early & I thought would insist upon seeing his stocking but he didn't & I dressed him as usual. and when we were all ready opened the door. you should have seen his

Caroline Frey Winne, 1867.
Courtesy New York State
Historical Association Library,
Cooperstown.

eyes stick out. The room looked like a toy shop and some of the things are beautiful of their kind—I never saw more Xmas giving then there has been here. Mr. Moore [the post trader] had a large assortment of very nice toys & fancy things. and then men have bought without limit. the Thomas children were loaded with beautiful things by the men of their fathers company. and laundress children too had no end of things.

Baby had nothing in that way of course except Sergeant Divine (Gussies [their servant girl's] husband) gave him a large & very handsome set of ten pins & a large humming top. and a man who lives with Major Upham bought him today a very pretty plated knife & fork. I was sorry to have either of them do it but they would have been greatly hurt if I refused their gifts.

. . .Saturday—The mail came in evening late—and brought your beautiful letter to Bopper. and another train of cars for him. he is delighted with his letter and sends a kiss to Uncle & Auntie. Much warmer this morning and all well.

Boppers Xmas Presents 1879:

Mamma & Papa—Beautiful saddle horse on wheels, set of nine pins, book—Under the Window, Whip, Driving reins with bells; Grandma Winne—Box building blocks, transparent slate, set of magnetic toys (fish & ducks), Chinese straw bird whistle; Mrs. Armsby—Wax doll, toy watch & chain, rubber ball, picture book— (Mother Hubbard), picture book—(4 & 20 Blackbirds); Mrs. Yiels, Albany—Magic Mother Goose Melodies, a beautiful book.

Gus—Book—Jennie Wren; Etta—Book—The Picture Alphabet; a lovely collar—Carries own work; Christmas Cards, Xmas tree book— Hoboken; Box of candy—father; Savings bank—Lieut Wheeler; Train of cars—Lieut. Waite; Mouth Organ—Capt. Forbush; Creedmoor bank—Major Upham.

Beautiful large wheel barrow & whip—Mrs. Moore; Tin market wagon & horses—Miss Moore; Large red, white, & blue ball and dog in a hoop—Gussie; Large set of ten pins & humming top—Sergeant Divine; Whip & card of paper soldiers—Mrs. Thomas; Knife & Fork—O'Grady; Train of Cars.[10]

It was not uncommon for children of popular military leaders, such as Benjamin Grierson, to receive special presents. Alice Kirk Grierson at Fort Concho, Texas, in 1875 recalled one such gift to her son, George.

> **A soldier gave George a pretty little brown puppy Christmas. George says it is a pointer and thinks a great deal of it.[11]**

Nine-year-old Carleton Allen lived with his family at Camp Steele, San Juan Island, Washington. His father, Major H. A. Allen, served with the Second Artillery. Carleton wrote to his cousin of the gifts he received for Christmas 1866.

> **We had a Christmas tree. I got a sword and gun, trumpet, riding whip, a dog whistle, 125 glass marbles, a ball, and other things.[12]**

Not all children were particularly gracious when it came to gifts, especially when one believed a special gift was going to another. Forrestine Cooper Hooker's reminiscence of Christmas 1873 at Fort Concho, written from a child's point of view, is a delightful example of how greed and pettiness could turn to utter delight.

> **Christmas of 1873 approached. So many officers were away on scouting duty that preparations for trees in various homes were abandoned. It was then that General Merritt and his wife, who had no children of their own, decided to have a Christmas tree in their home for all the children of the garrison. There were to be gifts for every child, and the families were to bring the home gifts for presentation at the same time. The Merritts had been very partial to me and many times had taken me to walk with them. I always hated walking, and I remember I could not see any sense in strolling on the prairie near the post when I was accustomed to riding my pony, Dobbin, for miles over the same places. One day, however, we had a real adventure. General Merritt discovered a rattlesnake, and I was permitted to help throw stones at it until it was dead.**
>
> **A week before the Christmas entertainment, I came in from a ride at an unexpected moment. Mrs. Gasman was in our front room with my mother. In the younger woman's lap was an enormous doll with china head, legs, and arms. Mrs. Gasman was making a dress of white swiss with many ruffles edged in narrow pink ribbon. I rushed to her side, demanding: "Are you dressing that doll for me?" "No," she replied, "It is for Bessie Constable." I glared at the doll, trying to see some defect in it, and when Mrs. Gasman continued, "Don't you think it is a beautiful doll?" I retorted scornfully, "No. It has**

three eyebrows." "But that black mark is its eyebrow, like yours, and the pink line is where it opens its eyes. The other black line is for the eyelashes," she explained. "I don't like dolls with three eyebrows, but maybe Bessie Constable won't mind it," I said.

I left the room hating Bessie Constable. I did not see the doll again until Christmas Eve when I discovered it hanging in a conspicuous place on the big tree in the Merritt's front room. I looked at it and glared at Bessie Constable, who had no idea how I disliked her. Finally the doll was lifted down by General Merritt, who was dressed as Santa Claus, and he slowly read, "For Birdie Cooper." My surprise caused a big laugh, for everyone knew about the three eyebrows. Too happy to even speak, I held the doll in my arms. Then Mrs. Gasman spoke: "Do you like it?" I replied that it was a wonderful doll, the prettiest doll in the whole world. "But it has three eyebrows," she went on without a smile. "I don't care how many eyebrows it has. Dolls ought to have three eyebrows!" Other gifts were handed to me, among them a beautiful silk scarf that Mrs. Merritt had brought from Paris and which later was worn as my best sash, but none pleased me so much as the china doll.[13]

Of course, children were not the only ones to receive gifts. Some adults recalled with similar delight the presents they received. Ephriam Goodale, a civilian whose son, Capt. Greenleaf Austin Goodale, Twenty-third Infantry, served at various posts in the frontier army, listed the gifts his son gave him for Christmas 1882 at Fort Bayard.

Christmas—Capt. G. and the boys had a good visit to Fort Bliss and Mexico and ret'd safely. Lots of presents this morning for self and boys. Letter and handkerchief from Carrie and one fr. Cousin Belle today. Greenleaf gave me 1 silk hkf., 1 silk necktie, 1 linen hkf., oranges, apples, cigars, etc. etc. All the officers and ladies interchanged presents in the most generous manner.[14]

Cynthia J. Capron, wife of Lt. Thaddeus H. Capron, Ninth Infantry, described gifts received by young and old alike at Fort Hartsuff, Nebraska, for Christmas in 1874.

> We had a very pleasant Christmas Eve. We had a nice pine tree loaded with bags of candy and popcorn and presents.
>
> I told Mary I would write to her all about the Christmas presents but if you will be so kind as to send this letter to her it will do instead.
>
> Captain and Mrs. Munson, and Mrs. Caine, Mr. Holliday, the post trader, Mr. Graham (he has charge of building here), and wife, and Joe, were the company. Joe and Mrs. Munson put the things on the tree while I dressed. I had been pretty busy for a week, I can tell you, and had no nurse girl.
>
> When the children were ready, Thad took Elo and Henry to the Doctor's, and Hazen went over to play cards with Emma till everything was ready. They were delighted when they saw the tree; Elo particularly so, when she saw there were two dolls.
>
> Thad had a set of shirt studs and a nice necktie from me, a box of cigars from Mr. Graham, and from Mr. Holliday half a dozen bottles of champaigne [sic] and sherry, a box of candies and one of cigars. I had from Thad a very pretty silver butter dish, from Mrs. Munson, a nice ivory handled silk fan. From Mr. Graham, Tennyson's Poems in one volume, which I prize very much.
>
> We told all beforehand it was a tree for the children and we wanted them to come and see it. We did not wish them to bring any presents, but they did as they pleased about that. It was so pleasant here that we did not need any fire, scarcely.[15]

Cynthia J. Capron. Courtesy American Heritage Center, University of Wyoming.

Dr. John V. Lauderdale, stationed at Fort Bridger, wrote in 1865 how pleased he was with receiving a surprise gift:

> Mrs. Carter commended my choice of her good things and took me very much by surprise by making me a beautiful christmas present. It was an highly embossed silver napkin ring with my name engraved upon it, which she had just received from New York.[16]

Julia Gilliss, wife of Capt. James Gilliss of the Quartermaster Department, recalled in a letter to her brother of "making do" with gifts available from the post sutler at Camp Warner, Oregon, in 1867.

> We have not yet got over Christmas frolics and I think of you all at home very much and hope you are having a nice time. We have enjoyed it very much, although we are too far away from town to buy anything for presents, yet we had some fun from that fact for we would go [to] the sutler's store and buy anything he happened to have. One lady got a dark calico dress, another got some cans of oysters; I got two bottles of perfume, a tin box of arrowroot, a pretty collar, a dozen eggs, and a couple of apples. Eggs & apples are almost worth their weight in gold out here, so they were valuable presents.[17]

Daniel Robinson, Seventh U.S. Infantry, fondly recalled the last Christmas at Fort Laramie. He retired as a captain in 1889, shortly before the army abandoned the grand old post. His nostalgic reminiscence recalled an abundance of gifts.

> It was now well into November, and Christmas was coming. I will venture to say that there is no place outside of an isolated military fort where the Christmas holidays are more appropriately and joyously observed, the preparations for which lay within the province of the ladies exclusively, about twelve or more, and grandly they did it.
>
> A large tree had to be found and placed in the hall at the proper time—large enough to hold presents for all, from the commanding officer down. It was much easier to get the tree than to obtain the decorations and gifts. A ladies meeting was held at which the first lady of the fort presided and the requisite funds provided. Catalogues had to be looked over and selections made. The ladies were all artists in music, painting, embroidery, rag doll and doll dress making, also in dainty refreshments; each and all undertook the parts they were most skilled in. Of course their husbands were interested, not in the way of suggestions, but to assist and obey without grumbling when called on by the lady managers, such as attending to the decoration of the hall and procuring the tree, the latter, a task that fell to the lot of the bachelors, who made frequent trips to the mountains to find a suitable one.
>
> The presents had all arrived from the east, the hall decorated with evergreens, flags, arms, the old battle flags of 1812, Mexico, and of the late war holding prominent places in front.

Christmas Eve had come, and with it the beautiful snow. The tree was placed in the hall, ornamented and loaded with gifts—a tree of beauty, sparkling like diamonds in the light of tiny wax tapers.

Santa Claus had also come, seated on his car of state at the foot of the tree. The tree was so high that a ladder had to be provided.

The hall was illuminated, the doors were opened, and the garrison had assembled.

From an adjoining room advanced the carol singers, composed of boys and girls dressed in costume, led by one of the lady managers, a celebrated vocalist. On they came singing and dancing around the tree to the music of the orchestra. Round and round they went again and again until the end, a fairy scene ever to be remembered.

Santa Claus nimbly stepped up the ladder and commenced distributing the gifts. The name of the recipient was written on each, and when called they stepped up to the tree and received it with an appropriate remark from Santa Claus that made the hall resound with laughter and merriment.

The private received a useful book, the commanding officer a tin sword, the soldier's child a pretty doll, and the officer's a rag doll. The last bride and the prospective bride, the gentle reminders of the present and future, and so on until the tree was denuded.

Refreshments were served all around; the lights on the tree began to flicker and burn out. Santa Claus bowed himself out amid a shower of well wishes and farewells to look after the little ones that were in bed and asleep dreaming of him. The assembly broke up and departed, happy and grateful for the favors received.

Many of the ladies had little responsibilities tucked away in blankets at home that were too young to participate in the festivities of the evening, all of whom had hung up their stockings, expecting Santa Claus to come down the chimneys during the night and fill them in accordance with the little notes on the hearth. The fond mothers, after returning from the hall, take a peep up the chimneys, look into the stockings, and see that everything is in proper order for the expected visitor. Besides all this there were little trees hid away in closets and out houses that had to be brought in and placed in the parlour, decorated and prepared at odd times during

the week, all ready to be lit up in the morning, covered with more toys and dolls than the little ones had ever seen before.

By daylight they were up and skirmishing around, looking into their stockings, which were found to be crammed full, and then the racket began. No more rest or sleep for anyone in the house after discovery. All night these children had been dreaming of Santa Claus, and now it was their turn to have a fine time.

The parlors were forbidden ground until after breakfast and then more surprises and fun. Later they could be seen running from house to house with Christmas cards, cards of congratulation and presents.

A Christmas feeling prevailed over everyone and everything, indoors and out. All military duties were suspended except guard. Officers met, smiled, and congratulated each other; then repaired to the office of the commanding officer to congratulate him.

Companies had big dinners that day, each vieing with the other to have the best. Hunting parties had been out, and they returned with antelope and deer. Turkies, and all that goes to make a Christmas feast, were abundantly supplied. But, this was not all; after tattoo a grand ball was given by the companies in the hop room, and everyone was invited, including all of the pretty ranch girls and their friends on the Laramie and Platte. It was quite a grand affair and conducted with more order and decorum than is often seen at more select affairs.[18]

Gifts even made their way to Fort Conger beyond the Arctic Circle in 1881 and caused great joy among the men as expedition leader Lt. Adolphus W. Greely recounted.

I had assigned to Sergeant Rice the grateful task of distributing the Christmas gifts, and he performed his duty with pleasant and well received remarks befitting the gift and the person receiving it. We had neglected to provide ourselves with a Christmas tree, and our new country afforded not even the semblance of a shrub, the largest plant—the creeping Arctic willow—being about a foot long and not over an inch above the surface of the ground. In consequence, the gifts were spread out on our largest table.

The thoughtful consideration of a few friends and well-wishers of the expedition, some of whom were personally unknown to any of us, had resulted in the donation of many

articles, both valuable and useful. Every officer and man received a package addressed to him personally, and some were sent for distribution at the discretion of the commanding officer. The idea was a most happy one, and it would have done the generous donor much good could they have known how much pleasure their gifts made in the hearts of the men who received them. A number of the men, who had lived lives marked by neglect and indifference on the part of the world, were touched even to tears, although they strove manlike, to conceal them. The commanding officer received a fan—not needed for Arctic use—and Lieutenant Kislingbury a small dog, which excited the more amusement when he turned away the ridicule by calling out, "Oh, Schneider, don't you want to buy a dog?" Poor Schneider did not hear the last of it for several days. The prosperity of the joke lay in the fact that Schneider had for many weeks devoted his spare time and attention to the successful raising of our Arctic puppies. These gifts were supplemented by a number from the commanding officer, which were distributed by lot, some of value and others of an amusing character. A plentiful supply of egg-nogg, and the removal of the restriction as to the hour of retiring, made the evening a delightful one, and long after the Sabbath and Christmas came together the quarters resounded to hymns, chants, carols, and sentimental songs.[19]

For Christmas 1885 at Fort Bayard, New Mexico, post residents devised a special method of distributing the gifts to the delight of all.

The event of the season, for which we have been preparing, and to which we have been looking forward for weeks, has taken place. It was a lottery Christmas tree.

Each lady furnished as many presents as there were members of the family—some furnishing for the bachelors. The presents for the ladies were numbered with even numbers, and those for the gentlemen with odd. The numbers were then put in two silk bags and passed around to the ladies and gentlemen and drawn, the present bearing the number corresponding to the one drawn from the bag being the gift of the person drawing it.[20]

For some on the frontier, even though stationed in locations where goods were available, ingenuity did not play a part and the old fallback gift—money—was sometimes suggested. Alice Kirk Grierson suggested to her son Charlie that it might be easier for him to procure his own present in a letter from Fort Davis in 1882.

If you can find anything in your travels that particularly suits your fancy for ten dollars, you can buy it for a Christmas present for yourself, and I will give you the money.[21]

Jennie Barnitz, though stationed with her husband Capt. Albert Barnitz, Seventh Cavalry, at Fort Leavenworth, where nearby shopping was substantial, wrote rather happily of her monetary gift.

Dec. 25, 1867. Christmas! Albert because he had no opportunity of getting me a Christmas present gave me a hundred dollar bill, which some day I will spend as I choose. It has been a quiet day. Even more quiet than Sunday. Albert did not want to go to church, & I did not insist.[22]

Emily McCorkle FitzGerald recalled the gift she received from her husband in 1874:

Doctor and I mourned together over not having anything for each other, but when I got up in the morning I found an envelope pinned to my pincushion with a twenty dollar gold piece in it. What pretty things they are! I have two now and mean to keep them to buy something pretty with.[23]

Notes

[1] Roe, *Army Letters from an Officer's Wife*, 23-24.

[2] Mrs. Orsemus Bronson Boyd, *Cavalry Life in Tent and Field* (New York: J. Selwin Tait & Sons, 1894), 224-25.

[3] Barbara E. Fisher, ed., "Forrestine Cooper Hooker's Notes and Memoirs on Army Life in the West, 1871-1876," Masters thesis, University of Arizona, Tucson, 1963, 89-90.

[4] FitzGerald, *Army Doctor's Wife*, 169-70.

[5] Ibid., 320-21.

[6] *Leavenworth Times*, Dec. 25, 1888.

[7] *ANJ*, Jan. 22, 1881.

[8] *Hays Republican*, Dec. 29, 1888.

[9] Capt. Simon Snyder, "Diaries from 1866 through the 1880s," Little Bighorn Battlefield National Monument, Crow Agency, Montana; quoted in Patricia Y. Stallard, *Glittering Misery: Dependents of the Indian Fighting Army* (San Rafael, Calif., and Fort Collins, Colo.: Presidio Press and The Old Army Press, 1978), 84.

[10] Thomas R. Buecker, ed., "Letters from a Post Surgeon's Wife," *Annals of Wyoming* 53 (Fall 1981):56-57.

[11] Shirley A. Leckie, ed., *The Colonel's Lady on the Western Frontier: The Correspondence of Alice Kirk Grierson* (Lincoln: University of Nebraska Press, 1989), 81.

[12] Allen Family Letters, from the research files of San Juan Island National Historic Park, Friday Harbor, Washington; this excerpt quoted courtesy the National Park Service.

[13] Fisher, "Forrestine Cooper Hooker's Notes and Memoirs," 122-24.

[14] Roy Goodale, ed., "A Civilian at Old Fort Bayard, 1881-1883," Roy Goodale, ed., *New Mexico Historical Review* 25 (Oct. 1950):301.

[15] Ted Stutheit, "Early-Day Holidays," *Nebraskaland* 59 (Dec. 1981):29.

[16] Lauderdale to his sister, Dec. 29, 1865, Lauderdale Collection.

[17] Gilliss, *So Far From Home*, 160-61.

[18] Daniel Robinson, "Reminiscences of Fort Laramie," manuscript, Special Collections, Fort Laramie National Historic Site, Fort Laramie, Wyoming.

[19] *Omaha Daily Bee*, Dec. 21, 1885.

[20] *ANJ*, Jan. 9, 1886.

[21] Leckie, *Colonel's Lady*, 154.

[22] Robert M. Utley, ed., *Life in Custer's Cavalry: Diaries and Letters of Albert and Jennie Barnitz, 1867-1868* (Lincoln: University of Nebraska Press, 1977), 132.

[23] FitzGerald, *Army Doctor's Wife*, 81.

Chapter Eight

SANTA CLAUS IS COMING TO THE FORT

"His advent through one of the windows was a great surprise. . ."

Father Christmas, a somewhat intimidating predecessor to our present image of Santa Claus.

The nineteenth century saw the evolution of the figure we call "Santa Claus." Our perception of Santa began with Father Christmas, who originated from both St. Nicholas and pagan predecessors. He often appeared in nineteenth-century illustrations wearing great fur robes, crowned with wreaths of holly, ivy, or mistletoe, and carrying a yule log or bowl of Christmas punch. Frequently, the public saw him with his hands clenched around switches, ready to punish naughty children, while lugging a huge sack of toys on his back for good ones. During the 1860s, however, artist Thomas Nast created our modern vision of Santa Claus in a series of drawings featured in the pages of *Harper's Weekly*. As Nast's jolly interpretation of Santa Claus captured the fancy of the American public, Father Christmas faded from view.

The frontier army had its own interpretations of Santa, yet he was always an important part of its holiday entertainment. An anonymous correspondent to the *Army and Navy Journal* told of Santa's 1871 arrival at Fort Lyon, Colorado.

After the usual services on Christmas day, preparations were made for a Christmas tree. Presents for the children had been procured from the East, and the tree was literally loaded

down with gifts. At six o'clock all assembled, and in the midst of some remarks by the chaplain in reply to the query as to who Santa Claus was, a veritable representation of that ubiquitous individual, covered with furs, and with a "jolly red nose" and marks upon his countenance suggesting an acquaintance with the interior of chimneys, appeared. He was greeted with shouts of laughter mingled with screams of terror from certain uninitiated juveniles whom he very soon conciliated, only, however, to a certain degree, as there was a very suspicious appearance of something indefinably terrible about him, the effect of which no

Artist Thomas Nast's cuddly interpretation of "Jolly Old St. Nick."

amount of candies or curious presents could entirely eradicate. After the distribution of the presents from the tree he disappeared and soon returned with his "pack upon his back," vastly increasing the merriment by the character of some of his presents—but we must close, earnestly hoping that the highly laudable suggestions conveyed by certain gifts of very small sized stockings and exceedingly diminutive red shoes may not be lost upon any who are "wasting their sweetness on the desert air."[1]

Santa made his way to Fort Omaha, Nebraska, in 1886.

At General and Mrs. Wheaton's invitation a number of children and grown people assembled to witness old Santa Claus and to experience his generosity. A slight delay, intensified by childish impatience, caused a variety of perplexities to arise in the juvenile fancy lest the jolly old Santa Claus had had his back broken by the weight of his pack or had been clogged in the chimney because of growing obesity. When the children, hand in hand, followed by their parents and elders, entered the spacious front room, a brilliant sight met their gaze. In the large bay window, all decorated with flags, was placed the Christmas tree. And such a sight it was! From floor to ceiling, thickly loaded with handsome presents for young and old, resplendent with gilt and tinsel and illuminated by myriads of wax tapers. Santa Claus was there true enough, and he advanced, all smiles to greet the children. In the task

of distributing his gifts Miss Kittie Miller, General Wheaton and Captain Dempsey lent their assistance. When the tree was lightened of its load and when each one in the room had received several reminders from Santa Claus, that beneficent body bowed himself out, saying as he departed that he must visit many other firesides that night.[2]

The jolly one also arrived at Fort Crawford, Colorado, in 1887 and proved that Santa was not strictly for children.

Early in December the men of both companies decided to join forces and organize a new club to be known as the "Merry Christmas," having for its sole object the preparing of a suitable place for the reception of "Santa Claus." Accordingly the good saint was communicated with; he not only consented to visit us but promised to do so quite early in the holiday season. The work of decoration was pushed forward so rapidly that 8 o'clock in the evening of the 23d found the preparations completed, and the entire command, both old and young, assembled in the post hall. An hour was spent in listening to some delightful music rendered by the post band; then the large flag that had been draped across the lower end of the hall was drawn aside and there was disclosed to our admiring gaze one of the most beautiful trees that I ever saw—every branch laden with presents and glittering with innumerable waxen lights. The merry jingle of sleigh bells was soon heard, and in an instant Santa Claus stood in our midst. With a few words of kindly greeting he turned to the tree and commenced his labor of love. In an incredible short space of time over 400 gifts had been distributed; then, with many kind wishes for the coming year, the good old man departed. No one had been forgotten; to the children he had been more than generous, each little one having everything requisite to begin housekeeping on a small scale. The ladies were each presented with an appropriate souvenir. Mrs. Hampson, Mrs. Mack, Mrs. Karbach and Mrs. Przykalla were the happy recipients of exquisite fans, the dainty handiwork of Miss Mack. "Santa" was particularly fortunate in his selection of gifts for the gentlemen; time and space will only allow me to enumerate a few of the most beautiful: Major Hampson, our popular post commander, was presented with an elegant ink stand, gold pen and pencil; Lieutenant Stottler, handsome cane; Dr. Worthington, a beautiful wax angel. This gift was quite a work of art as well as very appropriate, for

"Captain Santa Claus." From a short story by Charles King, the soldier-novelist.

when we have been afflicted with the various ills flesh is heir to, we have always found the doctor a ministering angel. Evidently "Santa Claus" sympathized with Lieutenants Paulding and Bateman, in their fondness for the "weed," for to each of these gentlemen was given a very handsome smoking set. It is useless for me to attempt to give a complete list of the many things, both useful and ornamental, that were given away by "Old Saint Nick;" suffice it to say that all were made happy. Soon after the departure of "Santa Claus" the officers and their families withdrew, leaving the hall to the "Merry Xmas" Club and their guests; about 12 an elegant lunch was served, after which we danced until the first notes of reveille called us to less agreeable but more exacting duties.[3]

The indomitable Santa even managed to reach the warmer frontier posts, such as Fort Davis, Texas, in 1886.

Dr. Paul Clendenin personated Santa Claus at the post Christmas tree very successfully and to the great gratification and delight of the little folks. His advent through one of the windows was a great surprise to them. His fur cap and coat, sprinkled with snow flakes, was abundant proof that he came from some far off climate, as they seemed quite out of place in this sunny land. But he explained the incongruity in a very satisfying manner.[4]

For Mary Leefe, daughter of 1st Lt. John G. Leefe, Nineteenth U.S. Infantry, stationed at Fort Dodge, Kansas, in 1878–80, attention focused on the garrison Christmas tree party. There was something distracting, yet vaguely familiar about Santa Claus.

The great tree, brilliantly lit with real candles and carefully watched by two enlisted men, stood upon the stage at one end. It seemed to our young eyes at least fifteen feet tall. The hall was painted white and lit by many kerosene lamps on brackets and central fixtures. It was festooned with garlands of evergreen and filled with the odor of burning wax candles. An orchestra of enlisted men furnished the music for dancing which was to follow the distribution of gifts. These were grouped about the tree and along the walls of the stage.

There were dolls, Noah's arks, animals, and every conceivable kind of toy for the kids, brought from afar on orders placed weeks before. But many of the toys were made by women of the fort [such as] dolls in complete costume, even to coats and hats. They had been made from dainty bits in the clothing of officers' and soldiers' wives. It is doubtful if any children of today get any greater thrill from their expensive mechanical toys than came to the tots on that far-off plain from something that had been made by the wife of Captain This or Sergeant That. . . .

What excitement when Santa Claus came in from a side door on the stage to distribute the gifts! I was so overcome with awe that I ran and hid behind the big bass viol. One of the musicians bid me not to be afraid and go up and get my gifts. I edged timidly up to Santa Claus. There was something funny about his eyes, they looked just like my daddy's. I was no longer afraid.

When the presents had all been distributed and Santa had retired, chorals were sung and the floor cleared for dancing. I ran to my mother with my presents and looked 'round for my daddy. He was nowhere to be seen, but shortly came out the side door through which Santa had disappeared. The children sat along the walls and watched the dancing begun by their elders. First, the commanding officer and his lady, then the other officers present, in order of rank, with their partners, followed by the noncommissioned officers in the same order down to and including the many private soldiers present, till the floor was filled. The children had their chance in an interlude, during which they were also treated to refreshments—popcorn, cake, and ice cream.

. . .Those among the elders who had no children and who so desired remained to pursue the dancing to a later hour. Outside all was still and the stars shone as they only can on a clear winter night on the plains. Someone struck up "Silent Night" and the various groups diverging on the paths leading to the officers' and married soldiers' quarters joined in, filling the stillness of the night with this sweet melody.[5]

Notes

[1] *ANJ,* Dec. 30, 1871.

[2] *ANR,* Jan. 8, 1887.

[3] Ibid., Jan. 7, 1888.

[4] Ibid., Jan. 8, 1887.

[5] Mary Leefe Laurence, *Daughter of the Regiment: Memoirs of a Childhood in the Frontier Army, 1878–1898,* ed. Thomas T. Smith (Lincoln: University of Nebraska Press, 1996), 28–29.

Chapter Nine

BRINGING CHRISTMAS TO THE INDIANS

"White man no bueno."

Few frontier army posts, stereotypes aside, were besieged by attacking warriors. Most were open, not pallisaded affairs, and, more often than not, located near tribal reservations. Indians appeared as frequent visitors, conducting a variety of business, and many garrisons shared their holiday with Native Americans living nearby. While one can argue the benefits and drawbacks of Indian-soldier contact, Christmas provided an opportunity for one culture to observe the other's celebrations. Whether it was because of Christian missionary zeal or the simple and generous good cheer of the season, frontier Christmas accounts prominently feature Indians, particularly Indian children.

Apache children observing Christmas at Fort Sill, Oklahoma Territory, 1898.
Courtesy U.S. Army Field Artillery and Fort Sill Museum.

Col. Homer W. Wheeler, while stationed at Fort Washakie, Wyoming, with the Fifth Cavalry in the late 1870s, recalled with some pride how he introduced the holiday to the Shoshone and Arapaho Indians.

> **I gave the Indians at my post their first Christmas tree. I asked the scouts to subscribe to the fund, which they did very liberally, so that every woman and child received a suitable present. I also gave each child a bag of nuts, candy, cakes and some kind of fruit. Moreover, I had Santa Claus come into camp with a sled loaded down with gifts. I then explained to them in simple words about the day and how Christmas originated. They never forgot that day and very often referred to it.[1]**

Martha Gray, daughter of Maj. Charles Carroll Gray, a physician with the U.S. Army Medical Corps stationed at Fort Stevenson, North Dakota, recalled the absence of Christmas presents in 1867 when no boat arrived. However, she happily played with toys she already had, some of which neighboring Indians had made. When the boat containing her Christmas presents finally arrived in April, her new doll created quite a sensation.

> **Our personal disappointment was great as my mother had counted on letters and the Christmas box from her family. But I do not remember missing them as I had my old toys and the little clay figures of animals made by the Indians, one in particular, a beautifully modeled buffalo, I remember. . .**
>
> **In April we saw the smoke of the first boat, our main link with civilization, and our Christmas mail was excitedly opened. Mine contained a wonderful wax doll with flaxen hair and with eyes which opened and closed and which I clutched and would hardly let out of my hands. Through Tonka Mary [the Gray's Indian servant] the Indians heard of my doll, and often while playing with it on the floor, the windows would be darkened, and I would look up to see dark faces peering in to look at "Waxy," as I called her. My father was offered buffalo skins, beaver pelts, and other valuable things for it, but I was never asked to make that sacrifice.[2]**

Marion Brown at Fort Sill in 1886 told her mother that Christmas hymns presented somewhat of a mystery to the Indians who gathered for the festivities.

> **The Christmas tree was quite a success. All the children, white, black and Indian had presents on it. Carrie sang a solo. Some of the Indians asked Mr. Jones, the interpreter, what the squaw was doing. He told them she was invoking the great Spirit to make the men's hearts better, that they may be**

> better to the squaws, that they would help them work and
> make their lives easyer [sic] and happy. It was a hymn on the
> birth of Christ. Quite a cute idea for Mr. J to interpret so. A
> number of Indians were squatted close around C. She said
> she could not keep from feeling frightened, they looked so
> big and silent. Each of us had a nice lot of candy on the tree.[3]

The 1866 Christmas season found some units of the frontier army in the midst of a war with the Sioux Indians. However, relations with other tribes were civil. Lt. George M. Templeton, stationed with the Eighteenth Infantry at Fort C. F. Smith in Montana Territory, recorded in his diary the effect of a popular winter pastime on Crow Indian allies living near the fort.

> Finished my skates and introduced skating on the Big-
> Horn. The skates are passingly good, but the ice is not.
> Several of the Indians looked on in silent wonder.[4]

Chief Washakie. NSHS R539:26 1.

Andrew S. Burt, 1888. Courtesy Fort Laramie National Historic Site.

Elizabeth Burt, 1862. Courtesy Fort Laramie National Historic Site.

Capt. Andrew S. Burt, Twenty-seventh Infantry, remembered his remarkable 1866 Christmas dinner with Chief Washakie, a stalwart Shoshone ally of the army, at Fort Bridger.

> At the appointed hour on Christmas day, Washakie and his
> "talk man" rang the bell of the front door and were ushered
> into the parlor where my wife and I were waiting to receive
> them; of course, the Indians had no hats or overcoats to
> deposit in the hall before their entrance. I received the Chief,
> shook hands with him and turned to my wife and went
> through the ceremony of presentation to Mrs. Burt. With
> extra elaborate politeness Washakie advanced, took her hand

and said: "How. I like your man. Glad see his wife." The talk man's keen little black eyes watched every move of his chief and his actions were as near like them as possible.

Mrs. Burt, Washakie and myself sat in the parlor chatting until dinner was announced. Upon acquainting Washakie with this fact, he arose in a dignified manner, turned and pulled his blanket around his shoulders, turning to do so in order that he might not expose his person, he being lightly clad in accordance with the Indian custom. He stood at complete ease until Mrs. Burt preceded us into the dining room, and upon a sign from me followed as if accustomed to such actions every day. In the dining room Mrs. Burt pointed out the seat he was to occupy and he stalked up to his chair but, to my utter amazement, he remained standing until Mrs. Burt took her seat at the head of the table when he pulled the chair from under the table and sat down. He remained perfectly passive awaiting Mrs. Burt's next move. Mrs. Burt removed the band from her napkin and placed it across her lap. He immediately did the same thing. Soup was served and I was anxious to see what he would do, for Indians have no regard for the silver and steel helps to eating in refined society, but again he did the right thing, picked up the soup spoon and ate as delicately as if he had been accustomed to it all his life. The same thing happened with his knife and fork as the turkey and other courses were served, and his dessert spoon came into use at the proper time. He took his after dinner coffee, used his finger bowl with a nicety and after Mrs. Burt had left the table joined me in a smoke and chat.[5]

Not all soldiers were as hospitable as Andy Burt. Members of Gen. Phil Sheridan's command, Department of the Missouri, seemed reluctant to share any holiday cheer with the local natives in 1868. Newspaper correspondent De B. Randolph Keim reported:

Christmas day, with its associations of home and winter recreation, was duly celebrated in camp. Milk punch, concocted of the condensed material, sugar, and Texas "spirits," was the popular beverage. With their usual facility of discovering everything that is going on, the leading warriors in the vicinity of camp in some way or other found out that the day was more than an ordinary affair. Resolved to convince themselves of the fact several delegations, painted and plumed, and mounted on their best war ponies, set out for the various headquarters. At the time at Hazen's tent a number

of officers were present. As the warriors came up, and heard the conversation within, they probably felt reassured that something was going on.

The chief of the party dismounted, and poking his head through the entrance of the tent, cast one hasty glance at the crowd of officers. The chief exclaimed "how?" and grinned invitingly. A chorus of "hows" were returned, but nothing further was said, notwithstanding the chief kept his feathered head in sight for some minutes.

After withdrawing his regal pate a half dozen other warriors got down from their ponies and gratified their curiosity by taking a peep.

Essahavit, war-chief of the Peneteghtkas [a band of the Comanche tribe], soon came along, and, bolder than the rest, entered the tent. A number of the other warriors followed him, and squatted in one corner, assuming their usual stolidity of countenance. Probably twenty minutes had elapsed, and all the officers except one or two had gone. Essahavit, unable to withstand the temptation, very methodically walked up to the improvised punch bowl—a horse bucket. He observed to the General, "bueno," at the same time evidently awaiting an invitation. After repeating this suggestion several times the old chief found his hints were not appreciated and left. The other warriors left also, observing as they filed out of the tent "white man no bueno."[6]

Katherine Gibson, wife of Capt. Francis M. Gibson, remembered the Seventh Cavalry enjoying its final Christmas of peace. Hers is a poignant and heart-warming tale, set at Fort Abraham Lincoln, Dakota Territory, in 1875. One can assess whether it had a greater impact on Mrs. Gibson or the Indian children.

When the last guest had departed, I thought I would take a peep into the kitchen, now dark and deserted, so, with lighted candle held high, I opened the door. As the flame stabbed through the blackness I suddenly gasped and gazed before me with startled eyes, for on the side porch appeared some strangers huddled together—strangers of juvenile stature, one barely tall enough to see above the window casement. In short, my uninvited guests were small Indian children, who were staring through the glass at the tree in mesmeric entrancement. For a moment I was held spellbound in surprise, then, cautiously, so as not to frighten them, I opened the porch door and motioned them to enter. At first they cowered and shrank away, then a straight-backed youngster

Mrs. Francis M. Gibson and baby Kate. Courtesy *With Custer's Cavalry* by Katherine Gibson Fougera. The Caxton Printers, Ltd., Caldwell, Idaho.

in buckskin, dragging by the hand a diminutive squaw about four years old, stepped into the room, the others following warily, single file. How had they gained entrance to the garrison, I wondered? Then I recalled a slight breach in the stockade wall, just big enough to admit the wriggling in and out of one small body at a time.

I turned to the supposed leader of the party and, speaking slowly, asked, pointing to the tree, "Someone tell Indian boy about it?"

He nodded, as the little hostiles around the agencies picked up a smattering of English very quickly.

"Who tell Indian boy?"

"Horn Toad."

Horn Toad was a good-natured Indian scout, adored by all the children in the garrison.

"Oh," I nodded, while the little frozen band huddled about the stove in stolid silence, "and who is she?" indicating the wee squaw.

"Sister," replied the boy, while the little girl clung more fiercely to his hand. My eyes ran over the tiny figure, and my heart contracted. The poor tot shivered and drew across the shoulders of her calico dress an impromptu shawl made of gunny sack, and a strip of the same material served as her only headgear. Her moccasins and leggings were of buckskin. The young warriors were clad in whole suits of it, but evidently, when it came to the females of the species, the supply

had given out. It was a miracle that the little band hadn't been frozen to death.

Just how, where, or why at this season of the year these people were abroad instead of being under shelter at the agencies did not matter. The fact remained that they and at least some of their tribe had set up their wickiups somewhere near by. I mentally shook myself. What an unconscionable hour for these children to be up. They must be returned to their mothers at once, and yet, as I looked into their timid, expectant faces, pity stirred within me, and my logic went woefully awry. Heaven only knew how long they had waited out there in the cold, feasting their eyes upon this glittering paradise, and that set me thinking. Quickly I drew them into the living room and towards the Christmas tree pie, which, I was confident, still held a few treasures, and, digging into the sand myself, I fished out a Jack-in-the-box which I presented to the little lady. Her black eyes leaped with surprise and joy, and her wee hands trembled as she clutched the toy. Then, making a motion for them to continue, I flew to the kitchen to heat up what cocoa still remained. The striker was just leaving for his barracks when I called to him.

"Oh, Alkorn," I instructed, "go to the nearest bastion and tell the sentinel to relay to other sentinels that, in the event of any Indians hanging around and looking for children, they are at Lieutenant Gibson's quarters and will be along soon."

During my absence my guests had certainly explored the entire contents of the tub. The appearance of the Jack-in-the-box had dissipated their last vestige of hesitation, and they plunged feverishly into the sand, and with each rag doll, toy pistol, or other treasure they exhumed, they became in fact wild Indians—wild with delight—the boys voicing their emotions in short grunts, the wee one in squeals of rapture.

It was upon this scene of oozing, scattering sand that I entered, bearing a pot of steaming cocoa, but the children refused to abandon the magic tub until the very last toy had been salvaged. Then they drank long and thirstily of the refreshing beverage, and soon color returned to their pinched cheeks and warmth crept back into their little chilled fingers. Noting all this, I communed with myself thoughtfully. I should have sent them home right away, I told myself severely, yet I continued to heap their laps with goodies, popcorn, nuts, and candy. Besides, there was some ice cream left over and cake, too, that were begging to be eaten, and

what was a party without them? So, before they knew it, mounds of pink and white concoction were whisked in front of the little savages, who immediately plunged small eager fingers into the pretty, fluffy stuff, only to recoil from the sudden chill. The tiny squaw was the first to experiment with it, by cautiously licking some off her palm, and her cherubic smile would have inspired a masterpiece from Raphael. They needed no further urging and attacked the ice cream, stuffing themselves with all the abandon of healthy, hungry children.

While they were thus engaged, I ran upstairs looking for old blankets, woolen stockings, and socks. I found a short coat of my own, some mittens and galoshes and warm mufflers. Suddenly queer sounds coming from below sent me scurrying halfway downstairs, where I paused. The noise started with the clapping of hands, accompanied by a weird chant. This was followed by the sound of softly muffled feet and short, sharp whoops, at first faint but growing louder and louder. I sank upon the stairs and peered through the bannisters into the living room, and what I beheld kept me rooted to the spot. My eyes dilated before a picturesque phase of barbaric expression.

The straight-backed boy, evidently wishing to do his part and that of his tribe toward the entertainment, was staging a performance of his own and was directing the others in some kind of dance. One boy and the diminutive squaw stood at the side clapping their hands and chanting monotonously, the latter moving her hips and body in imitation of the older squaws while, circling the stove in single file, the young braves stamped upon the carpet with the firmness of buffaloes combined with the whirlwind lightness of the wildcat, their lithe frames swaying like the prairie grasses and with a rhythm as perfect as a set measure. Backwards and forwards they flung themselves as though made of elastic rubber, bending pliant heads and necks and emitting long-drawn-out whoops of joy. The crunching into the carpet of ruinous sand mattered not, for on the step I sat like petrified wood, lost in wonder at the wild beauty and cadence of that native dance. Why, I pondered, did white children have to spend money to attain anything like the grace of these aborigines to whom it seemed as inborn and as natural as a spring of cool, pure water. The dirge changed, and the little redskins swung into close, group formation, each executing fast, fantastic steps.

Followed more insistent hand clapping and droning. The young bucks quickly flung back into single file, whereupon the dance became fiercer, the whoops louder and longer, and with a frenzy that almost shook the floor they fairly leaped about the stove until the leader held up his hand and stopped. The droning ceased, the embryo braves threw themselves, gasping, upon the carpet, and the wee one slid down beside the young chief.

I drew a deep breath, hurried back upstairs, and brought down an armful of clothing and blankets. Then I bundled up the wee squaw like a bale of cotton, tied my too-big mittens on her warm little hands, and gave the rest of the blankets, mufflers, and galoshes to the boys. After that I stripped the tree of its remaining gifts, put candy and cake in a bag, which I consigned to the care of the straight-backed boy, and very reluctantly let my guests out again into the night. I glanced up at the clock in the hall. Already it was Christmas. The snow crunched crisply beneath light retreating steps while again and again the happy children, clutching their cherished toys, turned radiant faces over their shoulders for one last look and smile.

Finally, the small, straight-backed Indian boy, bringing up the rear with his Christmas burdens, patted his mouth with his slim hand and emitted the farewell call of his tribe, which seemed to linger on the air even after the little band had faded from view.[7]

Notes

[1] Homer W. Wheeler, *Buffalo Days, Forty Years in the Old West: The Personal Narrative of a Cattleman, Indian Fighter and Army Officer* (Indianapolis: The Bobbs-Merrill Company, 1923), 326.

[2] Martha Gray Wales, "When I Was A Little Girl: Things I Remember From Living at Frontier Military Posts," Willard B. Pope, ed., *North Dakota History* 50 (Spring, 1983):15.

[3] King, *Letters From Fort Sill*, 37-38.

[4] Entry of Dec. 1866, George M. Templeton Diaries, quoted courtesy Everett D. Graff Collection, The Newberry Library.

[5] Mattes, *Indians, Infants, and Infantry*, 88.

[6] De B. Randolph Keim, *Sheridan's Troopers on the Border: A Winter Campaign on the Plains* (Philadelpia: David McKay, 1885), 171-72.

[7] Fougera, *With Custer's Cavalry*, 239-44.

Chapter Ten

ENTERTAINMENT

"All that is left to us are the recollections of a delightful party."

Christmas entertainment, those activities in addition to the usual feast, seemed to challenge members of the frontier army family and brought out their valiant efforts. Whether these endeavors were the result of nostalgia for the past, the need to escape the often brutal conditions and loneliness, or a special consideration for the children, the entertainment of which the frontier soldiers and their dependents partook was a veritable kaleidoscope of sights and sounds.

Kissing underneath the mistletoe, Fort Riley, Kansas. Courtesy Joseph J. Pennell Collection, Kansas Collection, University of Kansas Libraries.

The spectrum ranged from the simple singing of religious hymns to elaborate masked balls, from the enlisted man's robust tastes for athletics, well-fueled by post trader's whiskey, to the old army custom of firing a volley of joyous gunfire. While Christmas was one of the most sacred of Christian holidays, very few accounts mention deeply religious observances. In 1881 the population at Fort D.A. Russell, near Cheyenne, Wyoming, however, did focus on the religious aspects of the holiday with the singing of hymns.

> The Christmas tree at Fort Russell, Christmas Eve, for the Sunday school, was given under the direction of Mrs. James Simpson, assisted by Mrs. Steover and Mrs. Weldman, Lieutenants Ducat and Davis. The exercises opened with "Carol, Brothers, Carol," sung by the children followed by "Palm Branches," which was beautifully rendered by Major Sniffen, Mrs. Sniffen presiding at the organ. The children then sang, "We Three Kings of Orient Are." After singing "Silent Night," the curtain was taken down and the little ones beheld

Santa Claus standing by the Christmas tree, which was well filled with presents. Lieutenant Ducat acted his part as Santa Claus exceedingly well, and after the distributing of presents to each child, the little ones returned to their homes very happy. The officers and ladies spent the remainder of the evening very enjoyably in dancing.[1]

The garrison of Fort Shaw, Montana, also observed a more religious celebration in 1890.

The Christmas tree entertainment at Fort Shaw on Christmas Eve was a great success. The tree was beautifully decorated and were [sic] filled with appropriate presents for the little ones, who were present in full force and overflowing with joy and expectation. A large audience was in attendance, and, like the children, seemed to be joyous and happy and went to their homes feeling better for having been present. The exercises were about as follows: 1. Hymn, "All Hail the Power of Jesus' Name," by the audience. 2. Prayer by Post Chaplain Simpson. 3. Hymn, "Come all ye Faithful," by the children. 4. Lighting the tree. 5. Hymn, "Brightest and best of the Sons of the Morning," by the children. 6. Arrival of Santa Claus and presentation of gifts. 7. Passing of cake, nuts, etc., through the audience. 8. Hymn, "Come thou Almighty King," by the audience. 9. Benediction by the chaplain. So much was it enjoyed that some were heard to remark "I wish Christmas came every day."[2]

Lt. John Bigelow recounted his disappointment at not being able to go to religious services on Christmas Eve at Fort Davis, Texas, 1884.

Spent a pleasant Christmas. We spent the eve at the Gardner's. It was contemplated by the host and hostess that the party they would assemble would proceed at about midnight to the Mexican chapel to attend the Service, but through carelessness, I take it, the time was allowed to pass by and so that feature of the entertainment lost. Mary and I were rather disappointed.[3]

Plays and musical performances were often held throughout the year. At Christmas, special programs delighted all who attended, such as at this 1884 program at Fort Niobrara, Nebraska.

The little folks of the post gave a delightful theatrical entertainment on Christmas Eve, which was attended by all the big folks of the garrison. Opening address by Chaplain McAdam.

Fort Niobrara, Nebraska, after an 1888 blizzard. NSHS-A547:2-25.

The play entitled "The Pine Family" was rendered with the following cast of characters: "Pine Family," Miss Nellie Thomas, Miss Mollie Thomas, Master Willie McAdam, Master Henry Luhn; orphans, "Polly" and "Jack," Miss Georgie Thomas, Master Pherson Frazier; "Fairy Queen," Miss Maria Luhn; "Fairy Prince," Master Aubrey Lippincott; "Fairies," Miss Nan Sumner, Miss Kittie Thatcher; "Santa Claus," Mr. Becker.

The characters of "Polly" by Georgie Thomas and "Fairy Prince" by Aubrey Lippincott would compare favorably with the acting of older and more experienced performers, while the "Fairy Queen" and her assistants were so beautiful that the audience easily imagined them to be real fairies. The part of "Jack" was well performed by the Pherson Frazier, and "The Pine Family" and "Santa Claus" were excellent. The entertainment concluded with the distribution by "Santa Claus" of gifts from a fine Christmas tree, from which every child in the garrison received appropriate presents.[4]

Another form of Victorian entertainment popular on the frontier was the masked ball. Frances M. A. Roe gave another of her magnificent descriptions, this one from Fort Lyon, Colorado, in 1873. Note the superb creativity in the costumes.

Everyone in the garrison seems to be more or less in a state of collapse! The **bal masque** is over, the guests have departed, and all that is left to us now are the recollections of a delightful party that gave full return for our efforts to have it a success.

We did not dream that so many invitations would be accepted at far-away posts, that parties would come from Fort Leavenworth, Fort Riley, Fort Dodge, and Fort Wallace, for a long ambulance ride was necessary from each place. But we knew of their coming in time to make preparations for all, so there was no confusion or embarrassment. Every house on the officers' line was filled to overflowing and scarcely a corner left vacant.

Frances M. A. Roe and her dog, Hal.

The new hospital was simply perfect for an elaborate entertainment. The large ward made a grand ballroom, the corridors were charming for promenading, and, yes, flirting; the dining room and kitchen perfect for supper, and the office and other small rooms were a nice size for cloak rooms. Of course each one of these rooms, big and small, had to be furnished. In each dressing room was a toilet table fitted out with every little article that might possibly be needed during the evening, before and after the removal of masks. All this necessitated much planning, an immense amount of work, and the stripping of our own houses. But there were a good many of us, and the soldiers were cheerful assistants. I was on the supper committee, which really dwindled down to a committee of one at the very last, for I was left alone to put the finishing touches to the tables and to attend to other things. The vain creatures seemed more interested in their own toilets, and went home to beautify themselves.

The commanding officer kept one eye, and the quartermaster about a dozen eyes upon us while we were decorating, to see that no injury was done to the new building. But that watchfulness was unnecessary, for the many high windows made the fastening of flags an easy matter, as we draped them from the casing of one window to the casing of the next, which covered much of the cold, white walls and gave an air of warmth and cheeriness to the rooms. Accoutrements were hung everywhere, every bit of brass shining as only an enlisted man can make it shine, and the long infantry rifles with

fixed bayonets were "stacked" wherever they would not interfere with the dancing.

Much of the supper came from Kansas City—that is, the celery, fowls, and material for little cakes, ices, and so on—and the orchestra consisted of six musicians from the regimental band at Fort Riley. The floor of the ballroom was waxed perfectly, but it is hoped by some of us that much of the lightning will be taken from it before the hospital cots and attendants are moved in that ward.

Everybody was **en masque** and almost everyone wore fancy dress and some of the costumes were beautiful. The most striking figure in the rooms, perhaps, was Lieutenant Alden, who represented Death! He is very tall and very slender, and he had on a skintight suit of dark brown drilling, painted from crown to toe with thick white paint to represent the skeleton of a human being; even the mask that covered the entire head was perfect as a skull. The illusion was a great success, but it made one shiver to see the awful thing walking about, the grinning skull towering over the heads of the tallest. And ever at its side was a red devil, also tall, and so thin one wondered what held the bones together. This red thing had a long tail. The devil was Lieutenant Perkins, of course.

Faye and Doctor Dent were dressed precisely alike, as sailors, the doctor even wearing a pair of Faye's shoes. They had been very sly about the twin arrangement, which was really splendid, for they are just about the same size and have hair very much the same color. But smart as they were, I recognized Faye at once. The idea of anyone thinking I would not know him!

We had queens and milkmaids and flower girls galore, and black starry nights and silvery days, and all sorts of things, many of them very elegant. My old yellow silk, the two black lace flounces you gave me, and a real Spanish mantilla that Mrs. Rae happened to have with here, made a handsome costume for me as a Spanish lady. I wore almost all of the jewelry in the house; every piece of my own small amount and much of Mrs. Rae's, the nicest of all having been a pair of very large old-fashioned "hoop" earrings, set all around with brilliants. My comb was a home product, very showy, but better left to the imagination.

The dancing commenced at nine o'clock, and at twelve supper was served, when we unmasked, and after supper we

danced again and kept on dancing until five o'clock! Even then a few of us would have been willing to begin all over, for when again could we have such a ballroom with perfect floor and such excellent music to dance by? But with the new day came a new light and all was changed, much like the change of a ballet with a new calcium light, only ours was not beautifying, but most trying to tired, painted faces; and seeing each other we decided that we could not get home too fast. In a few days the hospital will be turned over to the post-surgeon, and the beautiful ward will be filled with iron cots and sick soldiers, and instead of delicate perfumes the odor of nauseous drugs will pervade every place.[5]

Those stationed at Fort Bayard, New Mexico, also hosted a masked ball to celebrate Christmas in 1887. This anonymous correspondent gave a bare-bones account.

Although the REGISTER does not very often hear from us down here in "No Man's Land No. 2," still we are alive, in a gratifying condition of robust health, and able to extract the maximum of pleasure from the opportunities offered. On the 26th a "motley crew," in masks, assembled in the hop room to celebrate Christmas in true style; and in the terpsichorean maze they tripped the light fantastic until the wee sma' hours. A good deal of originality was displayed in the choice of costumes. Among the participants in the hall were Major and Mrs. Cook, Petruchio and Katherine; Miss Devol; Captain Norvell, walking advertisement with local "hits;" Mrs. Norvell, Milkmaid; Miss Norvell, Little Bo peep; Captain Kendall, Uncle Hiram; Mrs. Kendall, Irish Girl; Mrs. Taylor, Captain Cavenaugh, Thirteenth Earl of Ruddygote; Mrs. Cavenaugh, Swiss Peasant; Assistant Surgeon Dietz, Paddy Duffy's "Unknown;" Lieutenant Stotsenburg, Little Boy Blue; Mrs. Stotsenburg, Kate Greenaway; Lieutenant Biddle, Scholar; Miss Biddle, German Peasant; Lieutenant Whipple, Jockey; Lieutenant Dade, Trovatore; Dr. Allen, Mother Hubbard; Mr. Booth, She; Mrs. Booth and Mrs. Posey, Two Orphans; Judge Posey, Mr. Copland, Wun Lung.[6]

Fort Snelling, Minnesota, witnessed a "fancy dress party" for Christmas 1890.

The holidays have come and gone, and they will long be remembered at Snelling as being unusually pleasant this year.

The small entertainment given Xmas night for the Sunday school children in the post hall, under the able management

of Col. Mason, passed off very nicely. Santa Claus (Capt. Wilkinson) and Mrs. Santa Claus (Miss Mason), distributed the presents. Tuesday afternoon Mrs. Kennedy gave a luncheon to the little girls in the post, ten in number. Capt. and Mrs. Hannay gave a small dinner Xmas Day. The informal hop Monday evening was, as usual, very pleasant. Wednesday evening Mrs. Winne gave a fancy dress party for her son Charley, who is home from Shattuck for his Xmas holidays. Some of the young ladies were invited to go in costume. Some of the costumes were as follows: The Misses Minnie Hobart, Liberty; Bessie Hannay, Tambourine Girl; May Jones, Popcorn Girl; Frances Mason, Folly; Mamie Williams, Poppy; Lydia Hobart, French Peasant; Bessie Williams, Japanese Girl; Julia Gerlach, Fille du Regiment. Little Miss Rosalie Williams as Little Bopeep, and Master Russell Jones as Little Boy Blue, attracted a great deal of attention. Miss May Mason wore a Swedish Peasant costume that she obtained when in Sweden summer before last and made a most fascinating peasant. Miss Jewett, who is a very handsome brunette, was excellent as an Indian Squaw. Her costume was very complete. The buckskin dress once belonged to the Nez Perce Indians. She wore a papoose cradle strapped on her back after the Indian fashion.[7]

Fort Buford, Dakota Territory, was the setting for an unusual "tissue paper hop" in 1887.

The ladies of the post gave a very successful tissue paper hop on Dec. 26 in the post hall, which was decorated very handsomely for the event by Mrs. J. A. Finley, Miss Crofton and Miss Murray, assisted by Lieutenant George W. Goode and Mr. T. A. Forbes. The decorations were greatly admired, being pronounced by several people the best ever seen in Fort Buford. Tissue paper of various colors formed the principal part of the display mingled with designs in flags, sabres and Chinese lanterns. The dresses of the ladies presented a gay and attractive spectacle in their wealth of color and elegance of make. Among the most noticeable were black and white, Mrs. T. Harley; black and orange, Miss Crofton; two shades of green, Mrs. J. A. Finley; pink and blue, Miss Murray; pink, Miss Maud Crofton; blue and white, Miss Wagner. All the above mentioned dresses were made entirely of tissue paper, but some of the other ladies only trimmed their dresses with that material. Nearly all, however, complied with the regulation of the evening in that respect.[8]

Other dances, were a bit quieter, as was this one at Fort Reno, Indian Territory, in 1888. The designation of a "hop room" reflected the importance of these activities to the post.

> **Christmas Eve was celebrated at the usually quiet little post by a delightful dance given in the hop room by Colonel and Mrs. Wade. At midnight the guests repaired to the commanding officer's house, where a handsome supper was served.[9]**

The soldiers themselves often provided the entertainment, several possessing surprising musical and theatrical talent. A group of Camp Sheridan, Nebraska, soldiers treated others at the post to a performance for Christmas 1880.

> **The "Camp Sheridan Minstrels" have issued their programme for Christmas night. The entertainment commences with the usual olio, then short sketches, entitled, "Electric Bath," "Grip Sack," and "Houlihan Musketeers," the whole to conclude with the laughable farce, "The Great Walking Match, or 1,000 miles in a 1,000 hours." Music and songs are interspersed. Christmas seems to be Christmas everywhere, and our soldiers honor and enjoy the day as much as any one.[10]**

Sarah E. Canfield, wife of 1st Lt. Andrew Nahum Canfield, Thirteenth Infantry, noted in her diary in 1867 the theatrical abilities of the men stationed at Camp Cooke, Montana Territory.

> **The winter is passing away. We have had little dinner dances and card parties to help pass the time. Some of the Soldiers formed a theatrical troupe [and] have an entertainment once a month. The one at Christmas was especially fine—Music, dancing and a short play. Some of the men had Seen a good deal of acting and had probably done Some work on the board.[11]**

Lt. Adolphus W. Greely, at an Arctic Circle camp, told of the talents of the Greely Expedition's variety show for Christmas 1881.

> **On the 26th the men were busy in the preparation for a variety show, which was set for that evening, as Christmas had fallen on Sunday. The Lime Juice Club announced that they would perform at the Dutch Island Opera House for one**

night only, and that dog-chariots could be ordered at 10 p.m. The admission fee was in tobacco, the current coin of Grinnell Land.

The first act was a representation of an Indian council, which ended with a war-dance. Nine of the party participated in this scene, which was admirably rendered. Most of the actors had served in the far west, and some had spent months continuously in Indian camps, and so were thoroughly familiar with the parts they portrayed. I doubt very much if a more realistic representation of the wild red man was ever presented in the Arctic Circle, if elsewhere.

A female impersonation followed, by Schneider, which afforded amusement for the party, but particularly so to the Eskimos. Schneider had provided himself at the Greenland ports with the entire costume of the Eskimo belle, and being a small man was able to squeeze himself into the garments. As he appeared on the scene with his elaborate make-up and closely- shaven face, one was struck by the excellent resemblance to the Innuit belles whom we had seen in lower latitudes. In his armoot, or woman's hood, he brought the largest of his charges, one of the Grinnell Land puppies, who was nearly frightened to death by the applause which greeted his first advent into polite society. Excellent comic songs by Henry were followed by equally amusing imitations of a well-known military character by Connell.[12]

An anonymous correspondent to the *Army and Navy Register* reported that Fort Totten, located in Dakota Territory, possessed a very entertaining minstrel troupe who performed for Christmas 1882.

The North Pole minstrel troupe early on Christmas night raised the curtain amidst the thundering applause of an over-crowded audience. So successful was the troupe in its undertaking that the playing of the "Black Statue" caused many a tear to trickle down the cheeks of many a fair dame and many a chicken-hearted youth. The music selections of the orchestra were, par excellence, the best ever known here, as was fully attested by the reiteration of encore by the audience. On Tuesday night the "Music Teacher in Trouble, or Sally's Revenge," won fresh laurels for the troupe. By it they have gained a lasting local fame that can be tarnished only by a series of blunders and mishaps, which, viewing present circumstances, are not likely to occur.[13]

Cavalryman H. H. McConnell, assigned to Buffalo Springs, Texas, recorded the singing of a nontraditional carol.

The approach of the Christmas holidays, 1867, seemed to influence the soldiers, and some preparations were made by the younger men to celebrate the occasion as best they could. I suppose there is no man—no matter how degraded or demoralized, no matter where he is, nor what his surroundings may be, if he can look back at all on his childhood days with any degree of pleasure—but who is more or less susceptible to the peculiar influences and memories of the Christmas-tide. Some of my men possessed a considerable degree of musical talent; in fact, I had three or four good musicians in my company, and these and some others formed a minstrel troupe, and with the aid of two violins, guitar, flute and banjo, made really good music. A vacant forage room was fitted up with a stage and seats, and on Christmas eve they gave an entertainment which was patronized by the whole garrison, from commanding officer to company cook. One Myers, a bugler in my company, and the life of the camp, brought down the house by singing the following original ode, written for him by myself and set to the then popular air of "Captain Jinks."

> I'm Private Blow of the U.S.A.,
> At first Bull Run I ran away;
> If I'd been killed that fatal day,
>   I wouldn't be now in the army.
> Of course I don't expect to fight,
> Want to fight, have to fight;
> Of course I neither drill nor fight,
>   While I'm in the regular army.

Spoken: No, my friends, you see I have so many other things to do, such as elevating the condition of the nigger, building the officers' quarters, etc., that I shall do but mighty little fighting.

> **Chorus:** For I'm Private Blow of the U.S.A.;
> Of course I live beyond my pay,
> For high and low that is the way
>   We do in the regular army.

> At first they sent me to Carlisle,
> They kept me there a little while;
> Since then I've footed many a mile,
>   A recruit in this regular army.

I thought, of course, I'd have a horse,
Ride a horse, an army horse;
I thought a trooper had a horse,
    To carry him through the army.

Spoken: But then, you see, I suppose they thought I couldn't ride; at any rate, I've had to walk so far in my cavalry service, for
    Chorus: I'm Private Blow, etc.

You ought to see the coat I wear,
And, then, the trousers, such a pair!
There's no such uniform, I swear,
    In any decent army.
I'll quit the "wearing of the blue,"
    When I get out of the army.

Spoken: Yes, my boy, if any over-solicitous tailor or shop-keeper ever says to me, "Oh! Mr. Blow, let me sell you this blue coat," I'll knock him over, and then explain my preju-dice against blue, for
    Chorus: I'm Private Blow, etc.

My sutler's bills come in so fast,
I fear I'll have to leave at last;
My credit days will then be past,
    When I get out of the army.
If Congress would but pass the bill,
Butler's bill, the army bill;
If Congress would but pass that bill,
    Then I'll get out of the army.

Spoken: And oh! Congress! your petitioners will ever pray, etc., for
    Chorus: I'm Private Blow, etc.[14]

Sporting events accompanied holiday entertainment, much like the events seen at Fourth of July celebrations. For those stationed where winter conditions could be brutal, activities were somewhat limited. The men of Fort Sidney, Nebraska, hosted an indoor boxing match for Christmas 1886.

The Sidney *Telegraph* gives us a piece of Army news a little out of the ordinary run. It says: The glove fight at White House Hall Christmas Eve between McCarty, of Company F, and Ryan, of Company E, Twenty-first Infantry, drew a huge audience of sportively-inclined gentlemen; it was interesting but short. Prof. Morrison and Mr. Patrick Bradley had on the gloves three rounds. Then came Anderson and McDonald, of the post, in a three-round contest. The principals appeared in the ring at 9:15, ready for the combat, which was to be with four-ounce gloves, London prize ring rules. J. E. Coffey was chosen referee and Harry Nolan time keeper. Maxwell seconded McCarty and Goodall and Bradley handled Ryan. When time was called both men stepped to the front and began a series of cautious walk arounds, each evidently a little afraid of the other. This was soon followed by lively fighting all around the ring and one or two claims of foul. In the eighth round Ryan retired to his corner claiming a foul. The claim was disallowed by the referee, who gave ten seconds for the ninth round to commence. Ryan again refusing to come forward, the fight was given to McCarty. Ryan has been drinking considerable the past month instead of training and was not in good condition. The men of his company knew this, and were not at all enthusiastic in backing, while on the other hand the Company F men cheered their favorite whenever he made a good play.[15]

It was always possible to overreach in the name of morale. Young Lt. John Bigelow, stationed in Arizona in 1885, was determined to initiate a Christmas field day for his men whether they wanted one or not.

This being Christmas day, I had no drill, and no duty but the necessary guard and fatigue duty. The horses, not being put on herd, were watered at nine o'clock instead of eight, the usual hour. At ten o'clock began a series of physical contests among the men, which I had arranged and prepared with no little trouble. I told first sergeant, the day before yesterday, that I wanted to have something of the kind on Christmas day, in lieu of drill, and told him to have some five or six men come to me as a committee. No one came. I asked the sergeant about it the next day, and was told that the men were great growlers, that very few seemed to care anything about my scheme; that Private — had seemed at first to take some interest in the matter, but finding himself detailed for guard on Christmas day, had seemed to lose it all. "Some of these

men, sir," said the sergeant, "if they go in for anything of the kind, will expect to be excused from duty for a week afterwards." Finding out from him that Cropper and Hazard were still interested, I sent for them, and with their aid drew up a programme of exercises. I then told them to get what men they could as competitors, and to let me know how many they got. About one o'clock, having then a small number, they informed me that some of the men wanted to know, before entering, whether there would be prizes, and that others said that they had enough exercise drilling (they have one drill a day); they did not want any running and jumping. I told my committee to go ahead and make the necessary preparations, and gave the corporal of fatigue orders to assist them.

Yesterday evening I drew up the final programme, as follows:

	Prize
One-fourth of a mile run	$1.00
200 yard dash	1.00
One mile walk	1.00
Straight running jump	1.00
Straight standing jump	.50
Hop, skip, and jump	.50
Running high jump	1.00
Three single jump	1.00
Tug-of-war	

The quarter of a mile run fell through; all the other contests, however, came off, many participating who had before shown no interest in them.[16]

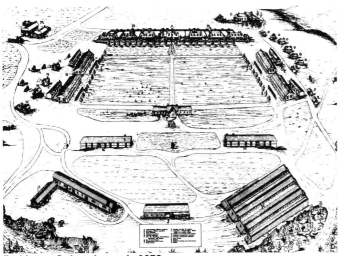

Fort Lyon, Colorado, early 1870s.

Fort Lyon, Colorado, fielded mule and pig races to celebrate Christmas 1873.

Slow mule race came off at 12 o'clock with the following entrees [sic]: Goldsmith Maid, Flora Temple, Lucy, Sensation, Longfellow, Harry Bassett, Occident, American Girl, Lady

Thorn, Mountain Boy, Prairie Snoozer, George Palmer and Connors. The race won in a straight heat by Flora Temple. Time 4:90. Hurdle, foot, and wheelbarrow races afforded much amusement.

The greased pig race was not quite what it ought to have been owing to some being too hoggish for the swine.[17]

Another contrasting description of the same Fort Lyon holiday appeared in the *Army and Navy Journal.*

A more pleasant holiday. . .has rarely been passed at an Army post, than that recently enjoyed at Fort Lyon. Immediately after guard-mounting a "fantastic conclave of august horribles" passed round the post, and was drawn up for review in front of the commanding officer's quarters. Mounted on halt, maimed, blind, and toothless Army mules, and garbed in the most grotesque costumes, the conclave formed no small feature of the day's entertainment. Among the notables in the processions were Robinson Corkscrew and his man Saturday, Captain Kidd, B. Franklin, and Joyce Heth.

The field sports, consisting of a "slow mule race," a hurdle (foot) race, a sack race, a wheelbarrow race, a foot race and the capture of a "greased pig"—were announced. The mule race and $5 were won by Floury Patesem, a cornfed Gothic, Government animal, with only a local reputation. The unguous matter from the exterior of the pig proved disastrous to the outer garments of about twenty of the contestants for his oleaginous embraces and especially so to the unmentionables of two or three ambitious officers. A few men, it was observed, imbibed an excess of Yule-tide patriotism; but, "Christmas comes but once a year," and why shouldn't they be merry? The masquerade ball in the evening was an affair long to be remembered by all present. Invitations were sent to all posts in the Department of the Missouri, and many foreigners honored us by their attendance. The costumes and disguises were all good, and several were quite original. Marie Antoinette and a Louis XIV courtier were present, also Brother Jonathan and three Virginius filibusters, a recruit and a crippled soldier, Night and Morning, Time and the Devil, etc., etc., with numerous dominoes ad hominem and ad womanem. The ladies of our very congenial little garrison deserve unlimited praise for the elegant supper they prepared; it could not have been excelled had the markets of New York been at hand. The decorations of the ball-room

were both tasteful and elegant, and the committee is hereby awarded honorable mention, which it is enjoined not to spent. The ball was closed by that "sound of reveille by night," and next day the parade ground was as deserted as a cavalry company after pay day. On the 28th our visitors were sent off with swell eyes and swell heads to duty and to ponder over the decreased estimates for the next fiscal year.[18]

Camp Verde, Arizona Territory, hosted a horse race for Christmas 1875. It proved to be the most civilized event of the day.

The first thing on the programe [sic] this morning was the horse race between Cos. I and E, for two hundred dollars a side, distance five hundred yards. Hats, boots and even Government socks were wagered on the race, and one man went so far as to bet his wife against ten dollars. I would have taken him up but my finances were rather low. Joe Conyers, 1st Sergeant Co. E, did the engineering work for E Co., and J. Murphy was acting in the same capacity for I Co. They are both undoubtedly excellent riders. The horses were entered at 10 o'clock directly after which the race commenced. Conyers keeping the lead from the very first, Murphy gained on him some at the latter end but of no avail. Conyers came out about 20 feet ahead, no time given. Immediately after, a rabbit was produced for a race but the poor fellow had been penned up so long that he was in no mood for running and the dogs got him before he hardly had time to get from his starting point.

In the evening we had a social dance accompanied by the A Co. string band. Everything seemed to be gratifying with all until a man of heretofore unblemished reputation jumped up and pulled off his coat with considerable hostility and made some ungentlemanly remarks which I do not wish to chronicle, and as a matter of course the young feminines got frightened and made straight way for their homes. Consequently the fandango was abandoned.[19]

Fort Stevens, Oregon, saw a few casualties result from a football game, still a relatively new sport in 1898.

The day after Christmas the Fort Stevens football team played against the Astorians. Pvt. Lewis, of Battery M, had his knee badly injured, and was carried to the hospital, where he will have to remain for several weeks. One of the Astoria team broke a leg and was taken home on a stretcher.[20]

Gen. George Crook, commander of the Department of the Platte, hosted a unique sort of entertainment for the day. The telephone, upon which we rely so heavily today to communicate with our loved ones at Christmastime, was a brand new invention, just appearing in Omaha, Nebraska, in 1877.

> A telephonic entertainment was given on Thursday evening between the residence of Gen. George Crook, Davenport and 18th streets, and the office of Gen. King, post commandant at Omaha Barracks. Gen. Crook's house was connected by special wire with the telegraph line between this city and the Barracks, and a special wire was run from the Barracks terminus of the line to Gen. King's office. The instrument used was the Bell telephone. . . .
>
> Among those at Gen. Crook's residence were Gen. Robert Williams and wife, Major Thornburg and wife, Major Furay and wife, Captain Nickerson and wife, Mrs. G. H. Collins, Lieutenant Schuyler, Lieutenant Bourke, Dr. Somers, Dr. Coffman, J. D. Iler, A. S. Patrick, Matt. Patrick, F. B. Knight, and others, besides the members of Gen. Crook's family, consisting of himself and wife, Mrs. Daily, mother of Mrs. Crook, and Mr. and Mrs. Reed, the latter being a sister of Mrs. Crook.

Gen. Crook (seated, center) **and staff, Department of the Platte, Omaha.** NSHS-A741-148.

In Gen. King's office were Gen. King and wife, Dr. Page and wife, Major Burt, Lieut. Stembel and wife, Lieut. Hays, Mr. Dickey, Mr. Korty, and others.

The programme was impromptu, and not only comprised vocal and instrumental selections, but also a conversation in the Crow language between Gen. Crook and Major Burt. The entertainment was entirely successful, and continued from 7 to 10 p.m. It is expected that telephonic communication will be opened soon between the department headquarters in this city and the barracks.[21]

Another unusual diversion for Omaha residents at Christmas, 1881, was an exhibition hosted by Lt. John G. Bourke, Crook's aide-de-camp.

December 24th, 1881. Saturday, Christmas Eve. I held an exhibition of Indian bric a brac at Gen. Crook's H'd Qrs., 10th and Farnham [sic] Sts., Omaha, Neb., to which came very many of my friends from among the people of the city; the officers of Fort Omaha not being able to reach town on account of the mud.[22]

Notes

[1] *ANR,* Jan. 7, 1882.

[2] Ibid., Jan. 3, 1891.

[3] McChristian, *Garrison Tangles,* 34.

[4] *ANR,* Jan. 3, 1885.

[5] Roe, *Army Letters,* 142-45.

[6] *ANR,* Jan. 14, 1888.

[7] *ANJ,* Jan. 24, 1891.

[8] *ANR,* Jan. 14, 1888.

[9] Ibid., Jan. 19, 1889.

[10] *ANJ,* Dec. 27, 1880.

[11] Ray H. Mattison, ed., "An Army Wife on the Upper Missouri: The Diary of Sarah E. Canfield, 1866-1868," *North Dakota History* 20 (Oct. 1953):215.

[12] *Omaha Daily Bee,* Dec. 21, 1885.

[13] *ANR,* Jan. 13, 1883.

[14] McConnell, *Five Years a Cavalryman,* 133-34.

[15] *ANR,* Jan. 2, 1886.

[16] Bigelow, *On the Bloody Trail of Geronimo,* 99-100.

[17] *The Colorado Prospector,* Dec. 1973, which reprinted the original story from a Las Animas, Colorado, newspaper.

[18] *ANJ,* Jan. 10, 1874.

[19] *Arizona Miner,* Jan. 7, 1876.

[20] *ANJ,* Jan. 7, 1899.

[21] *Omaha Daily Republican,* Dec. 22, 1877. Today we traditionally say "hello" when answering the telephone. It is quite likely that Generals Crook and King took a dim view to Mr. Bell's suggestion of a hailing word, "Ahoy!"

[22] Bourke diary, no. 54, 1881.

THREE TALES TOLD

"Even the officers were willing to help."

Christmas has always lent itself to the writing of great stories. Charles King, an invalided officer of the frontier army, became a popular novelist who frequently included Christmas material in his fiction. However, nothing that King invented equals our final three selections for humor, vitality, and drama.

Louisa Frederici Cody, wife of scout William F. "Buffalo Bill" Cody, fondly remembered Christmas in 1869 at Fort McPherson, Nebraska. Her "Will" played a central role in the post's entertainment, much to her chagrin.

However, right then, there were things to take Will's mind off the loss of his favorite pony. One of them was the fact that midwinter had come and that Christmas was only a few weeks off. For Will had been deputized by the soldiers and officers to be the official messenger who should go to Cheyenne and return with the necessities of the Christmas season.

And what excitement there was about it all! In that great camp, where lived the men who guarded the West, were only three children—three girls, the bandleader's child, Mrs. MacDonald's little girl, and Arta. And for them the soldiers had saved their money that they might have a real Christmas, and Will was to be the official messenger to Santa Claus.

I'll never forget all the conferences that were held. Night after night, Mrs. MacDonald in her little cabin, the bandleader's wife up at the fort, and myself, would lead the thoughts of our children

Louisa Cody. Courtesy Buffalo Bill Ranch State Historical Park, North Platte, Nebraska.

around to Christmas, that we might learn the things they most desired. Certainly that was not a hard thing to do, and one by one we gained the information we sought. Some of their wishes were entirely beyond the range of possibility—but where is the child who does not desire the impossible? And so it was with Arta and her two little comrades.

However, at last Will made his start toward Cheyenne, with the whole long list, and with a face that was longer. He was

Buffalo Bill Cody, about 1872.
NSHS-C671-150.

going to face that worst of ordeals—shopping. However, he was brave about it.

"Don't know what they're going to say when I walk in out there and ask for chiney dolls and all those other things out of Godey's Lady's Book," he announced. "But I'll do my best. I'll bring back the bacon or bust!"

And so he rode away, while we three women turned our attention to the plans for the Christmas day entertainment.

Of course, there must be speaking, and each of us picked out the piece we wanted our little girls to recite. I chose "The Star of Bethlehem," and night after night, while Will was away, I trained Arta in her recitation, outlining each little gesture, showing her how to emphasize every word. I was terribly proud of her, for I felt that her piece would be the prettiest of all—and, well, you know the natural pride of a mother.

Therefore, it was with glowing eyes that I greeted Will when he came back from Cheyenne, loaded down with packages, to say nothing of the wagon which followed him. It was two days before Christmas. Up at the fort the soldiers had been working, sending out details into the plains to find the prettiest little pine trees possible, to be placed about the big assembly hall—and I knew that the whole setting would be wonderful for my little triumph.

So, when Will had shown me all the presents he had brought for Arta from the big trading post, the rag dolls, the bright bits of silk, the little train of cars and the inevitable fire engine; the wooly dog and the other gee-gaws that had found their way into the Far West, I told him of my accomplishment. Then I added:

"Now, Will"—I stuffed the copy of the poem into his hand—"you'll just have to look after the final training. If Arta doesn't study right up until the last minute, she'll be just like all other children. She'll get up there to speak her piece and then won't remember it. That would be awful, wouldn't it?"

"Sure would," he agreed earnestly. "But why don't you do the rehearsin'?"

"Because, silly, I'll have to work up at the hall. My good-ness, all those soldiers have been piling stuff in there for a week, and land only knows what we're going to do with it! They think that all there is to fixing up Christmas decorations is to go out somewhere and cut down a tree. Only women can look after those things properly; besides, there's the popcorn to string and the trees to decorate, and everything like that! Gracious, we'll be worked to death looking after everything, to say nothing of all the cooking to 'tend to. And you haven't a blessed thing to do—so you can just finish teaching Arta that recitation."

"But suppose the Injuns break out?" he asked lugubriously.

"Well, that'll be different. But, so far, they haven't broken out, and, Will, you've just got to help me. Now won't you?"

He bobbed his head with sudden acquiescence, and began to stare at the paper which I had shoved into his hand.

"I'll start to-morrow," he promised faithfully.

The next morning I went to the fort to help the other women with the decorations for our first really big Christmas on the plains.

How we worked! How we schemed and contrived to make that big hall look like a Christmas back home! All in one day, there was everything to do—and very little to do it with. This was different from the land of civilization. There was no store to run to for an armful of tinsel, no decorator's shops to furnish holly and mistletoe and Christmas wreaths. The wreaths that hung upon the walls we made ourselves. The bright red berries that spotted them here and there were hard-rolled bits of red paper; the greenery everywhere had come fresh from the buttes and knolls of the plains, with here and there a few cactus spines thrown in to make things more difficult.

The popcorn had long lain in the bins at Charlie Mac-Donald's trading-post. It burnt, it parched, it did everything but pop. A hand-picked proposition was every puffy ball which went upon the strings, gleaned from skillets full of brown, burned kernels that had persistently refused to pop, to do anything in fact but scorch and smoke and instigate coughing and sneezing. But we were determined to have a regulation Christmas, and a few difficulties were not going to stop us.

All day long we worked, and far into the night, hanging the various bits of greenery, cooking on the old range that

slumped in one end of the hall, or decorating the trees. The soldiers, gawking here and there about the big room, did their best to help us, but where is the man who is a particle of good at Christmastide? Every time we would make a gain on the popcorn, one of them would come along and steal a handful, and then we would have to run them all out of the hall, laughing in spite of our vexation, and start all over. We knew the feeling in the hearts of those

The Codys—Arta, Will, and Louisa. Courtesy Buffalo Bill Historical Center, Cody, Wyoming.

men—they were children again, children back home, preparing for Christmas!

Late into the night we cooked and slaved, while our husbands waited for us, in a nodding line at one side of the hall. At last it all was nearly done, and with Will I started home.

"How did Arta get along with her piece today?" I asked.

"Oh, fine!" Will looked straight ahead. "I taught her and taught her."

"She won't forget it?"

"No sirree! She's got it down line for line."

I went to bed happy and expectant. Arta would look so sweet to-morrow. Will had brought her a pretty little plaid

dress from Cheyenne that fitted her wonderfully well, considering that a man had picked it out. Of course, there was the necessity for a little taking up here and a little letting out there, but I could get up early in the morning and do that before time to hurry to the hall again.

So at dawn I was at work and, finally, to awaken Will with breakfast and with the information that he must be the one to dress Arta and bring her to the hall. I would be working there until the very last minute, and I simply wouldn't have time to come back to the house. Will did not object.

"I'll have her dressed up like all get out!" was his cheerful announcement. "I sure want her to make that speech to-day!"

"And so do I. Goodness, won't it be just too lovely if she's the best one there?"

"If?" my husband questioned. "Why, there ain't any doubt about it. I bet Arta gets more hand-clappin' and shoutin' and that sort of thing when she does her little trick than both of those other children put together. Now, just you watch her! I'm handling that end of it and she's got all those lines down pat!"

"Well, don't you forget to go over it two or three times," I ordered as I kissed him and hurried to the door.

"Oh, we'll go over it a lot of times!" he assured me. "Just wait 'til you hear it!"

I rushed to the hall, again to work, again to scheme and devise. Then, somewhat flustered, I seated myself as the time for the entertainment approached and the soldiers thumped into the hall. Will, dressed in his usual buckskin and flannel shirt, found me sitting near the rear of the long lines of chairs and immediately assisted me to my feet.

"What?" he asked. "Sitting back here? No sirree! We're going right up with the mourners!"

"Mourners?"

"Well, you know what I mean. Up on the front row where everybody can see us when Arta makes that speech. Got it all down pat, haven't you, Arta?" He beamed down at her.

"Yes, Papa," she lisped, and a feeling of great pride swelled through me. Up to the front row we went, while the hall filled, and the Santa Claus of the fort, resplendent in a red flannel shirt hanging straight from the waist, a pair of riding boots that reached above his knees, and cotton whiskers and hair, filched from the post surgeon, distributed the presents. One

after another they were called out, first the presents for the children, and then the ones for the soldiers. There were paper dolls and baby rattles and a hundred and one foolish things that Will had bought in Cheyenne and packed across the weary miles; bottles of beer with vinegar in them, tiny kegs labeled in chalk: "Finest Whisky," and disclosing when opened only carpet tacks, and everything else foolish that men can think of. One by one they were all doled out, and then, following the booming of the post quartette, the singing of a solo by the band-leader's wife, and a speech on Christmas by the Major, the recitations began.

Mrs. MacDonald's little girl came first, and had I not known what a really wonderful presentation Arta would make, I would have been really jealous. Then followed the band-leader's daughter, with her little recitation, and then—

Arta!

Her father carried her up to the platform, squared her around, patted her on the cheeks and hurried back to his seat. My heart thumped with excitement. It was Arta's first recitation. Prettily she made her little curtsy, and then, with a quick glance toward her father, she parted her lips.

But the words that came forth! My pride changed to apprehension and then to wildest dismay. For Arta was reciting something that I never heard before, something only a few lines in length, that ran:

> The lightning roared,
> The thunder flashed,
> And broke my mother's teapot
> A-l-l t-o s-m-a-s-h!

Then she laughed, clapped her little hands and, running to her father, leaped into his lap. Will was almost rolling off his chair. The tears were running down his cheeks, his face was as red as a boiled beet and he was shaking with laughter from head to foot. As for the rest of the big hall, it was roaring like a summer thunderstorm, while I, like Cardinal Wolsey, sat alone in my fallen greatness. For a moment there was only blank dismay. Then I looked at Will and understood.

"Willie!" I exclaimed dramatically, "I'll never speak to you again as long as I live. Never! Never! Never!"

But a moment later, as he choked down his laughter, to boom out a lump-de-de-lump to the tune of "Rock of Ages," the closing song of the celebration, I reached over, took his

hand, squeezed it—then pressed tight my lips to keep from laughing myself. But never again did I trust to Will the task of rehearsing a child in its recitations![1]

Mary Rippey Heistand, wife of Lt. Henry O. S. Heistand, Eleventh Infantry, reminisced at length in 1907 of one Christmas Eve (probably 1880) at the cantonment on Poplar River, Montana. She summed up the importance of the garrison as an extended family.

It is not always the comforts of our modern garrison life that contribute most largely to our happiness and contentment. There comes to me a delight in the memory of past pleasures experienced amid surroundings primitive indeed if compared with those of the present day army life.

As the holiday season approaches there comes vividly to my mind one of the most delightful recollections of Christmas cheer that I have in my gallery of reminiscences of the old frontier life.

News came to our station, Fort Custer, Montana, that the Indians near the British border threatened an uprising. It was the old story we had heard so often. The agent and others at Fort Peck Agency, Poplar River, became so alarmed that they hastily left the agency. With the news came orders for us to immediately proceed to the scene of trouble. Accordingly, within a few days, two companies of the Eleventh Infantry, "B" and "F," were packed and ready to leave the post with all their household belongings and personal effects. When we started on the march our faces were headed toward we knew not what, except that it was to be a new home which we were to construct with such materials as the country afforded. How long or short would be our stay, no one knew.

. . .At last our situation made known at headquarters, nine troops of mounted Infantry and two troops of Cavalry from Fort Keogh; and a troop of Cavalry and a detachment of Infantry from Fort Buford, were sent to our relief. I shall never forget the sight they presented on their arrival just at dusk on Christmas eve.

The air was clear with the great still cold when the weary riders made their appearance. The sweat on the faces, shoul-

ders and flanks of the ponies had frozen, until from the uniform white of their appearance they seemed all to be of one color as they strung out in the early twilight. The cheer of hearty welcome with which we greeted the newcomers must have warmed their hearts almost as much as their appearance cheered us.

All the available dry wood to be had was turned over to them; and soon the bright glow of camp fires lessened the gloom of the bitter Winter night. The mercury was actually frozen, yet the relieving troops had no shelter but the tents they had brought with them on the march.

It was the beautiful army custom in those days for the officers already at the station to call the first evening upon the new arrivals. Accordingly our officers visited the tents that were put up in military precision close as convenient to our little shacks. Afterward all the new officers, most of whom I had already met, called to pay their respects to the two ladies in this little beleaguered post they had endured so much to relieve.

It was not much like a holiday gathering that Christmas Eve. They came dressed in the best that their limited kits afforded. (Winter campaigns in Montana were far from being pleasure trips.) Several of them were suffering from frozen noses, ears, cheeks or fingers, from the terrible exposure of the past week's ride. The painful peeling process was exceedingly annoying; but not a word of complaint was heard.

Realizing how hard it was for them to be away from their wives and families under such trying circumstances, and especially at this time of year that stands for family reunions, I invited ten of them for Christmas dinner the next day. It was my pleasure to take all possible pains to make my dinner attractive, and the subsequent delight of the home-hungry men fully repaid me.

. . .For the Christmas dinner, several tables were put together in the small dining room, almost filling it.

Despite their unpleasant and decidedly uncomfortable situation, all the guests appeared with the bright holiday faces that their beautiful optimism and gentle courtesy prompted.

Covers were laid for twelve, and as we entered the dining-room the guests stood still with appreciation at the sight of the table. I had procured from the trader, who had cared for them until we had entered our shacks, several geranium

plants; and by Christmas their buds had opened into warm
red flowers. They were at that bleak season a delight.

When the officers saw that the dinner preparations were
more elaborate than could have been hoped for in that out-
of-the-way place, their faces brightened still more, and as the
evening progressed my heart warmed to see that the spirit
of Christmas was assisting my anxious hospitality in causing
them to forget themselves and enjoy the present as much
as possible.

Our first course was raw oysters, which were canned and
frozen before shipment. For it I had made careful preparation. My man had cut for me a large square block of ice and
twelve small ones. With hammer and chisel and the aid of a
dishpan and a baking-powder can filled with boiling water,
these were transformed into receptacles for the sea food. A
hot flat-iron made for them all bevelled edges, and the large
block was further decorated with our monogram. The whole
gave a beautiful crystal effect. The novelty delighted the
guests and immediately dispelled the traces of sadness that
threatened. In fact, the ice dishes most effectually broke the
social ice, and started a warmth of approbation and comfort
in the little dinner.

The diary I have kept all my life brings back to me even the
menu of that night. After the oysters came soup, home-made,
and not the canned variety with which we had become so
familiar as diners on the frontier. Then followed salmon
croquettes with egg sauce and potatoes. The butcher had
provided me with sweet-breads, and these were served in
patties with peas fresh—from the can.

Too isolated for the Christmas turkey, we had a big roast of
beef, and I really do not believe the guests gave one passing
thought to the holiday bird. Potatoes and cabbage a la cauli-
flower completed that course. Prairie chickens and currant
jelly tarts melted from view before the canned asparagus salad
made its appearance; and no hostess ever had more reason to
be gratified by the enthusiasm with which each dish was
received, than I had upon that occasion. Cheese and crackers
preceded the sherbet, home-made cake, and the candies I had
made with hurried zeal.

Before the coffee had entirely disappeared, the room was
comfortably perfumed with cigar smoke; and the party was
launched upon after-dinner stories. We had been three hours

and a half at table, and were now quite in the humor for music and lively conversation.

One of the officers was an accomplished musician, and of course delighted with the presence of the piano. Solo, duet, chorus, story and instrumental duet followed each other in happy succession for a couple of hours after.

But the time for good-nights abruptly reminded us that this was the last social gathering before the impending fight with the Indians, which their insolent and threatening dispositions made inevitable. The idea entered every mind that the coming week might find us beyond earthly pleasures, and, as we were separated from all those we held dear in this world, it was impossible to escape a little depression. Since there are no sorrowful incidents to remember in connection with the fight, however, the recollection of our momentary depression does not dim that of the Christmas cheer.

One of the officers came to me just before they returned to their cheerless tents and the look upon his face wrung my heart. He had been unusually quiet for some time; but with true soul bravery and unselfishness, had tried to hide his feelings for fear of casting gloom upon the party. Now he came to me and said in low tones:

"I want to ask a favor of you, Mrs. H. If—if I should not get back again, and you see my wife and babies, will you tell them that I thought of them to the last?" Then, as though ashamed of the tears that hung heavy in his eyes, and the fear in his heart for those he left behind, he squared his shoulders and added in a voice that vainly tried to express optimism:

"But I'll be back, I'll be back."

Two other guests quietly asked me to take care of their wills, for of course we two ladies with the children would be protected to the last, and our goods would be safer than the guarded effects of the officers. And so my big trunk received into its safekeeping two wills; and I was charged with more than one last message.

Then with courageous hearts and bravely smiling faces, the Christmas guests took leave. It was an unusual holiday feast in every way, and the possibilities that the future held did not tend to make it less so; but I am glad to add that the dinner was not the last that we enjoyed together. The Indians were overcome with greater dispatch than expected, and without any fatalities on our side; had it been otherwise my memory

would have been of sorrow. Every one of that evening's party was spared to gather among their own for many subsequent "Merry Christmases;" and to partake of "Peace on earth, good-will toward men."[2]

Our final offering is a tale that could take its place alongside many better known events at Fort Robinson, Nebraska. Fort Robinson lies in the heart of the Pine Ridge country and stood as a guardian to the great Sioux reservations. The fort and its garrisons witnessed the majestic surrender and pointless death of Crazy Horse, the tragedy of the Cheyenne Outbreak, the unease of the nearby Ghost Dance, and the triumph of the epic marches of Guy V. Henry's buffalo soldiers. It was rarely a dull place and remains today a magnificent reminder of the past.

Our story can be found in a June 30, 1934, letter from Martin J. Weber to the editor of *Winners of the West,* the newspaper of veterans of the Indian Wars. It seems written almost as a modest afterthought. Yet it is a story of initiative, courage, and even humor, an illustration of the lengths to which some soldiers went to ensure a happy Christmas and of the memories an old soldier wished to record for history.

December 1882 then a Corporal in Troop "H", Fifth Cavalry, I was ordered on detached Service by the Commanding Officer. My orders were to report to the Quartermaster at Ft. Sidney the nearest railroad point to get the Christmas goods for the Fort. A driver and a six mule team were detailed for the purpose.

We started about December 10, a six days' journey. The weather was ideal, clear, sunny days and we arrived at Ft. Sidney on time but were delayed two days owing to the non-arrival of the goods that was coming over the Union Pacific Railroad. They finally arrived the morning of the 18th. We loaded our wagon at once and pulled out for Ft. Robinson one hundred and twenty-five miles to the North. The weather had turned cold and frost began to fly thru the air indicating a storm. We made good time that first afternoon camping just before dark. The next morning the storm broke in all its fury, a regular blizzard raging. We had to face or head into the storm. We made camp Clark where the Sidney Black Hills trail crossed the Platte river. A toll bridge, general store and

Post Office being kept at this point. Here we obtained shelter for ourselves, mules and horses.

The lady had a hot breakfast and coffee ready for us about daybreak. The storm had increased during the night. I mailed a report of the storm and that we would try and make the Fort if possible to the Commanding Officer. The Bridge tender and his wife advised us to

Facing a blizzard on the Great Plains. Engraving by Frederic Remington from *Harper's Weekly*, Aug. 13, 1892. Courtesy Frederic Remington Art Museum, Ogdensburg, New York.

stay until the storm should pass as they did not think we could travel in such a blizzard. As much as we disliked to leave the snug quarters and hot meals (we were to enjoy for the next three days only a ration of frozen bread and bacon), we bid them goodbye and headed into the storm. Without shelter or fire, three days and two nights, when we thot each day would be our last, we traveled over an open country for about fifty miles and had to break trail all the way, it being 30 to 40 degrees below zero.

The mules were going home, was the only reason we were able to make them face the blizzard. We had plenty of corn and oats for mules and the horses and at night we tied them so the wagon would act as a wind break and covered them with blanket lined covers. We would spread our tent on the snow, roll out our bed and pull part of the tent over us and let the storm howl.

We got to the stage station on the Running Water after dark the night of the 23d. Here we had hay for mules and horses and a good fire and warm place to cook our supper. How good that hot coffee tasted. The stage for the Black Hills and Deadwood arrived about 3 a.m., the first in three days. The Stock tender awakened us at 4 a.m. and had the coffee hot. It gave us new life and courage for the last twenty miles of our journey.

The stage had broke the trail to the top of Breakneck Hill, the storm had passed, the sky cleared, the sun shown bright and the Valley of the White River lay before us. The Fort was only five miles away. We got safely down the Breakneck, crossed White Clay Creek and broke trail across the valley arriving at the Fort about 2 o'clock, the afternoon of the 24th.

I rode ahead to report to the Commanding Officer. When I passed the Officers quarters the kiddies were all out running up and down the walks for the first time in 5 days having been housed up on account of the storm. When they saw me they began to shout, "The Christmas Wagon Has Come." The officers and men hearing them came out and asked if it was true. They could hardly believe it until the teamster drove his six weary mules up and we began to unload the Christmas goods. Even the officers were willing to help.

So old Santa arrived and there was a Merry Christmas after all had given up hope of seeing the Christmas wagon or Santa. A rocking horse was one of the presents for one of the youngsters who is now a Colonel in Washington, D.C. I was snow blind and had to wear dark glasses for some time after that trip.

One year later I was promoted to First Sergeant of Troop H.[3]

Notes

[1] Louisa Frederici Cody and Courtney Ryley Cooper, *Memories of Buffalo Bill* (New York: D. Appleton and Company, 1920), 196-206.

[2] Mary Rippey Heistand, "Scraps from an Army Woman's Diary," *Army and Navy Life,* Dec. 1907: 626, 629, 630-31.

[3] "Christmas 1882 at Fort Robinson, Nebraska: Bucking a Western Blizzard," *Winners of the West,* June 1934.

BIBLIOGRAPHY

Manuscripts

Allen, Carleton. Allen Family Letters. San Juan Island National Historic Park, Friday Harbor, Washington.

Bourke, John G. Diary, 1872-96. United States Military Academy Library, West Point.

Burt, Andrew S. Burt Collection. United States Army Military History Institute, Carlisle Barracks.

Corbusier, Fanny. Journal. The Corbusier Archives, Santa Fe.

Corliss, Augustus Whittemore. Diaries. Denver Public Library.

Dodge, Richard Irving. Papers. Everett D. Graff Collection, The Newberry Library, Chicago.

Larson, Robert R. "Christmas and New Year's Holidays on the Wyoming Frontier." Fort Laramie National Historic Site, Fort Laramie.

Lauderdale, John Vance. Collection. Beinecke Rare Book and Manuscript Library, Western Americana Collection, Yale University, New Haven.

McGillycuddy, Fanny. "Exact Copy of a Notebook Kept by Dr. V. T. McGillycuddy, M.D., while a Member of the Yellowstone and Big Horn Expedition, May 26-Dec. 13, 1876, and Notes Kept by His Wife, Fanny, at Camp Robinson, Dec. 13, 1876-Feb. 22, 1877." Typescript. Fort Robinson Museum, Crawford, Nebraska.

Robinson, Daniel. "Reminiscences of Fort Laramie." Special Collections, Fort Laramie National Historic Site, Fort Laramie.

Snyder, Simon. "Diaries from 1866 through the 1880s." Little Bighorn Battlefield National Monument, Crow Agency, Montana.

Templeton, George M. Diaries. Everett D. Graff Collection, The Newberry Library, Chicago.

Vogdes, Ada A. Journal, 1868-71. The Henry H. Huntington Library, San Marino, California.

Thesis/Dissertation

Fisher, Barbara E. "Forrestine Cooper Hooker's Notes and Memoirs on Army Life in the West, 1871-1876." Master's thesis, University of Arizona, Tucson, 1963.

Toll, Larry A. "The Military Community on the Western Frontier, 1866-1898." Ph.D. diss., Ball State University, Muncie, 1990.

Newspapers and Periodicals

Arizona Miner

Army and Navy Journal

Army and Navy Register

Bismarck Tribune

Cheyenne Daily Leader

Colorado Prospector

Harper's Weekly

Hays Republican

Leavenworth Times

Omaha Daily Bee

Omaha Daily Herald

Omaha Republican

St. Paul Pioneer-Press

Winners of the West

Books

Agnew, James B. *Eggnog Riot: The Christmas Mutiny at West Point.* San Rafael, Calif.: The Presidio Press, 1979.

Baur, John E. *Christmas on the American Frontier 1800-1900.* Caldwell, Ida.: The Caxton Printers, Ltd., 1961.

Bigelow, John, Jr. *On the Bloody Trail of Geronimo,* Arthur Woodward, ed. Los Angeles: Westernlore Press, 1958.

Bourke, John G. *On the Border with Crook.* Lincoln: University of Nebraska Press, 1971.

———. *MacKenzie's Last Fight with the Cheyennes: A Winter Campaign in Wyoming and Montana.* Bellevue, Nebr.: The Old Army Press, 1970.

Boyd, Mrs. Orsemus Bronson. *Cavalry Life in Tent and Field.* New York: J. Selwin Tait & Sons, 1894.

Brown, Dee. *The Gentle Tamers: Women of the Old Wild West.* Lincoln: University of Nebraska Press, 1968.

Carrington, Frances C. *My Army Life: A Soldier's Wife at Fort Phil Kearny.* Boulder, Colo.: Pruett Publishing Company, 1990; originally published as *My Army Life and the Fort Phil Kearney Massacre.* Philadelphia: J. B. Lippincott Company, 1911.

Carrington, Margaret I. *Ab-sa-ra-ka, Home of the Crows: Being the Experience of an Officer's Wife on the Plains.* Philadelphia: J. B. Lippincott & Co., 1869.

Carroll, John M., ed. *The Unpublished Papers of the Order of Indian Wars Book No. 10.* New Brunswick, N.J.: Privately Published, 1977.

Chalmers, Irena, et.al. *The Great American Christmas Almanac.* New York: Viking Penguin Inc., 1988.

Cody, Louisa Frederici and Courtney Ryley Cooper. *Memories of Buffalo Bill.* New York: D. Appleton and Company, 1920.

Commissary General of Subsistence, *Manual for Army Cooks.* Washington: Government Printing Office, 1896.

Corbusier, William T. *Verde to San Carlos: Recollec-*

tions of a Famous Army Surgeon and His Observant Family on the Western Frontier 1869-1886. Tucson: Dale Stuart King, 1969.

Custer, Elizabeth B. *Following the Guidon.* Lincoln: University of Nebraska Press, 1994.

Davis, William C. *The Civil War Cookbook.* Philadelphia: Courage Books, 1993.

FitzGerald, Emily McCorkle. *An Army Doctor's Wife on the Frontier: The Letters of Emily McCorkle FitzGerald from Alaska and the Far West, 1874-1878.* Pittsburgh: University of Pittsburgh Press, 1962.

Fougera, Katherine Gibson. *With Custer's Cavalry.* Caldwell, Ida.: The Caxton Printers, Ltd., 1942.

Frazer, Robert W. *Forts of the West.* Norman: University of Oklahoma Press, 1965.

Gilliss, Julia. *So Far From Home: An Army Bride on the Western Frontier, 1865-1869,* Priscilla Knuth, ed. Portland: Oregon Historical Society Press, 1993.

Howe, M. A. DeWolfe. *The Life and Labors of Bishop Hare.* New York: Sturgis & Walton Company, 1913.

Kane, Lucile M., trans. and ed., *Military Life in Dakota: The Journal of Philippe Regis de Trobriand.* St. Paul: The Alvord Memorial Commission, 1951.

Keim, De B. Randolph. *Sheridan's Troopers on the Border: A Winter Campaign on the Plains.* Philadelphia: David McKay, 1885.

King, C. Richard, ed. *Marion T. Brown: Letters From Fort Sill, 1886-1887.* Austin: The Encino Press, 1970.

Knight, Oliver. *Life and Manners in the Frontier Army.* Norman: University of Oklahoma Press, 1978.

Lane, Lydia Spencer. *I Married a Soldier.* Albuquerque: University of New Mexico Press, 1987.

Laurence, Mary Leefe, *Daughter of the Regiment: Memoirs of a Childhood in the Frontier Army, 1878–1898,* Thomas T. Smith, ed. Lincoln: University of Nebraska Press, 1996.

Leckie, Shirley A., ed. *The Colonel's Lady on the Western Frontier: The Correspondence of Alice Kirk Grierson.* Lincoln: University of Nebraska Press, 1989.

Mattes, Merrill J. *Indians, Infants and Infantry: Andrew and Elizabeth Burt on the Frontier.* Denver: The Old West Publishing Company, 1960.

McChristian, Douglas C. *Garrison Tangles in the Friendless Tenth: The Journal of First Lieutenant John Bigelow, Jr., Fort Davis, Texas.* Mattituck, N.Y.: J. M. Carroll & Company, 1985.

McConnell, H. H. *Five Years a Cavalryman; or, Sketches of Regular Army Life on the Texas Frontier, Twenty Odd Years Ago.* Freeport, N.Y.: Books for Libraries Press, 1970.

Monnett, John H. *A Rocky Mountain Christmas.* Boulder, Colo.: Pruett Publishing Company, 1987.

Myres, Sandra L., ed. *Cavalry Wife: The Diary of Eveline M. Alexander, 1866-1867.* College Station: Texas A&M University Press, 1977.

Oliva, Leo E. *Fort Union and the Frontier Army in the Southwest.* Santa Fe: Division of History, Southwest Cultural Resources Center, National Park Service, 1993.

O'Neil, Sunny. *The Gift of Christmas Past: A Return to Victorian Traditions.* Nashville: American Association for State and Local History, 1981.

Prucha, Francis Paul. *A Guide to the Military Posts of the United States, 1789-1895.* Madison: State Historical Society of Wisconsin, 1964.

Reed, Bill. *The Last Bugle Call: A History of Fort McDowell, Arizona Territory, 1865-1890.* Parsons, W.Va.: McClain Printing Company, 1977.

Reiter, Joan Swallow. *The Old West: The Women.* Alexandria, Va.: Time-Life Books Inc., 1978.

Remington, Frederic. *Pony Tracks.* Norman: University of Oklahoma Press, 1961.

Rickey, Don, Jr. *Forty Miles a Day on Beans and Hay: The Enlisted Soldier Fighting the Indian Wars.* Norman: University of Oklahoma Press, 1963.

Riley, Glenda. *The Female Frontier: A Comparative View of Women on the Prairie and the Plains.* Lawrence: University Press of Kansas, 1988.

Roe, Frances M. A. *Army Letters from an Officer's Wife, 1871-1888.* Lincoln: University of Nebraska Press, 1981.

Smith, Sherry L. *Sagebrush Soldier: Private William Earl Smith's View of the Sioux War of 1876.* Norman: University of Oklahoma Press, 1989.

Smith, Thomas T., ed. *A Dose of Frontier Soldiering: The Memoirs of Corporal E. A. Bode, Frontier Regular Infantry, 1877-1882.* Lincoln: University of Nebraska Press, 1994.

Spotts, David L. *Campaigning With Custer and the Nineteenth Kansas Volunteer Cavalry on the Washita Campaign, 1868-'69,* E. A. Brininstool, ed. Los Angeles: Wetzel Publishing Company, 1928.

Stallard, Patricia Y. *Glittering Misery: Dependents of the Indian Fighting Army.* San Rafael, Calif., and Fort Collins, Colo.: Presidio Press and The Old Army Press, 1978.

Utley, Robert M. *Frontier Regulars: The United States Army and the Indian, 1866-1891.* Lincoln: University of Nebraska Press, 1973.

——, ed. *Soldier and Brave: Historic Places Associated with Indian Affairs and the Indian Wars in the Trans-Mississippi West.* Washington: National Park Service, 1971.

——, ed. *Life in Custer's Cavalry: Diaries and Letters of Albert and Jennie Barnitz, 1867-1868.* Lincoln: University of Nebraska Press, 1977.

Werner, Herman. *On the Western Frontier with the United States Cavalry Fifty Years Ago.* Privately published, 1934.

Wheeler, Homer W. *Buffalo Days, Forty Years in the Old West: The Personal Narrative of a Cattleman, Indian Fighter and Army Officer.* Indianapolis: The Bobbs-Merrill Company, 1923.

Whitman, S. E. *The Troopers: An Informal History of the Plains Cavalry, 1865-1890.* New York: Hastings House Publishers, 1962.

Williams, Mary L., ed. *An Army Wife's Cookbook.* Tucson: Southwest Parks and Monuments Association, 1972.

Wooster, Robert. *Soldiers, Sutlers, and Settlers: Garrison Life on the Texas Frontier.* College Station: Texas A&M University Press, 1987.

Articles

Adams, Donald K., ed. "The Journal of Ada A. Vogdes, 1868-1871." *Montana The Magazine of Western History* 13 (July 1963):2-17.

Bingham, Anne E. "Sixteen Years on a Kansas Farm, 1870-1886." *Collections of the Kansas State Historical Society, 1919-1922,* 15 (1923):501-23.

Buecker, Thomas R., ed. "The Journals of James S. McClellan, 1st Sgt., Co. H, 3rd Cavalry." *Annals of Wyoming* 57 (Spring 1985):21-35.

——, ed. "Letters of Caroline Frey Winne from Sidney Barracks and Fort McPherson, Nebraska, 1874-1878." *Nebraska History* 62 (Spring 1981): 1-46.

——, ed. "Letters from a Post Surgeon's Wife: The Fort Washakie Correspondence of Caroline Frey Winne, May 1879-May 1880." *Annals of Wyoming* 53 (Fall 1981):44-63.

Carriker, Robert C., ed. "Thompson McFadden's Diary of an Indian Campaign, 1874." *Southwestern Historical Quarterly* 75 (Oct. 1971):198-232.

Eastman, Elaine Goodale. "Christmas Among the Ghost-Dancers." *The Midland Monthly* 2 (Dec. 1894):435-38.

Elting, John R. "Artillery Punch: A Study in American Degeneracy." *Military Collector & Historian: Journal of The Company of Military Historians* 27 (Spring 1975): 35–36.

Goodale, Roy, ed. "A Civilian at Old Fort Bayard 1881-1883." *New Mexico Historical Review* 25 (Oct. 1950):296-304.

Gressley, Gene M., ed. "A Soldier with Crook: The Letters of Henry R. Porter." *Montana The Magazine of Western History* 8 (July 1958):33-47.

Heistand, Mary Rippey. "Scraps from an Army Woman's Diary." *Army and Navy Life,* Dec. 1907:626-31.

Hill, Michael D., and Ben Innis, eds. "The Fort Buford Diary of Private Sanford, 1876-1877." *North Dakota History* 52 (Summer 1985):2-40.

King, Charles. "Captain Santa Claus." *Campaigning with Crook and Stories of Army Life.* New York: Harper & Brothers, 1890.

Lindberg, Christer, ed. "Foreigners in Action at Wounded Knee." *Nebraska History* 71 (Fall 1990):170-81.

Mattison, Ray H., ed. "An Army Wife on the Upper Missouri: The Diary of Sarah E. Canfield, 1866-1868." *North Dakota History* 20 (Oct. 1953):190-220.

——, ed. "The Diary of Surgeon Washington Matthews, Fort Rice, D.T." *North Dakota History* 21 (Jan.-Apr., 1954):5-74.

Morgan, Thisba Houston. "Reminiscences of My Days in the Land of the Ogallala Sioux." *South Dakota Department of History Report and Historical Collections* 29 (1958):21-62.

Peterson, Walter F., ed. "Christmas on the Plains." *The American West: Magazine of the Western History Association* 1 (Fall 1964):53-57.

Shirk, George H. "Campaigning with Sheridan: A Farrier's Diary." *The Chronicles of Oklahoma* 37 (Spring 1959):68-105.

Spring, Agnes Wright, ed. "An Army Wife Comes West: Letters of Catharine Wever Collins (1863-1864)." *The Colorado Magazine* 31 (Oct. 1954): 241-73.

Stutheit, Ted. "Early-Day Holidays." *Nebraskaland* 59 (Dec. 1981):24-29.

Taylor, Joe F., ed. "The Indian Campaign on the Staked Plains, 1874-1875: Military Correspondence from War Department Adjutant General's Office, File 2815-1874." *Panhandle-Plains Historical Review* 34,35 (1961,1962):1-368.

Wales, Martha Gray. "When I Was A Little Girl: Things I Remember From Living at Frontier Military Posts," Willard B. Pope, ed. *North Dakota History* 50 (Spring 1983):12-22.

INDEX